A Small Boat Guide to the
RULES OF THE ROAD

John Mellor

Fernhurst Books

To Des Sleightholme
for his help and encouragement when I first began writing

© copyright John Mellor 1990

First published in 1990 by Fernhurst Books,
33 Grand Parade, Brighton, East Sussex, BN2 2QA

British Library Cataloguing in Publication Data
Mellor, John, *1945–*
   A small boat guide to the rule of the road.
   1. Ships. Collisions. Prevention
   I. Title   II. Series
   623.8884

   ISBN 0-906754-54-2

All rights reserved. No part of this publication may be reproduced,
stored in a retrieval system or transmitted in any form or by any means
electronic, mechanical, photocopying, recording or otherwise,
without the prior permission of the publisher.

Printed and bound in Great Britain

Acknowledgements
The publishers would like to thank Dick Hewitt for his help and advice
when preparing the book. The text for pages 59–64 has been taken
from IMO's 'International Conference on the Revision of the
International Regulations for Preventing Collisions at Sea, 1972', also
referred to as Collision Regulations, with kind permission from the
publisher, the International Maritime Organization.

Photographs
The photographs on the pages indicated were supplied by the
following individuals or agencies:
Janet Harber: 30, 32
Tim Hore: 26
Motor Boat & Yachting: 4, 5, 21, 25
John Woodward: 7
Yachting Photographics: 19

Edited and designed by John Woodward
Cover design by Joyce Chester
Artwork by PanTek, Maidstone
Composition by Central Southern Typesetters, Hove
Printed by Ebenezer Baylis & Son Ltd, Worcester

CONTENTS

INTRODUCTION

The International Regulations for Preventing Collision at Sea, otherwise known as Colregs or Rules of the Road, are of vital importance to all sailors. They are also complex and wide-ranging, and not at all easy to remember. The main reason for this is the very precise wording necessary to avoid any confusion as to the meaning of each rule.

In this book we have simplified the whole subject to help you both understand and remember the essential information. However, the sequence of the rules has been followed faithfully. Each section is cross-referenced to the relevant rule, so that the information in this book can be easily compared with the precise wording of the rules themselves, which can be found at the back of the book. To prevent confusion we recommend that you do not do this until after you have thoroughly assimilated all the information given in the text.

Each rule, or group of associated rules, is presented on a page or double page spread, with illustrations where helpful. Each spread presents not only the necessary factual information contained in the rules covered, but also practical advice on the interpretation and use of them at sea in a small boat. We have also contrived a variety of mnemonics to help with memorising rules and lights.

The lights and shapes shown by vessels for identification are presented in groups according to the types of vessel and their rights of way under the rules. These groupings of related lights and vessels make them very much easier to identify and remember. Each type of vessel is accompanied by a description and an illustration of the lights carried, a description of the daymark (shape) shown, and a simple technique or mnemonic for remembering them.

In addition there is a section covering International Code Flags and single letter meanings – together with morse code and the phonetic alphabet – because certain code flags are used with their single letter meanings as daymarks.

Small vessels

It is important to bear in mind that the rules are written for commercial shipping rather than small boats. Small boats are catered for, certainly, and there should be no doubt, within the framework of the rules, as to how every type of vessel stands in relation to every other type in all circumstances. Neither should there be any confusion regarding the lights and shapes that should be displayed by small vessels.

At sea, however, especially in anything other than calm, clear weather, it is often extremely difficult for the most conscientious of lookouts to see a small boat before it gets too close for safety. It is also quite possible

that a large vessel will be reluctant to go to all the trouble of altering course for a small one if it can be avoided. She may well hold on till the last minute in the hope of bluffing you, before finally altering course according to the rules. This may be too close for your nerves, although perfectly legitimate (just).

Equally, with the accurate equipment and easy working conditions at his disposal the man on the bridge may calculate that he will pass comfortably and safely clear of you, at a distance which may also be too close for your nerves – especially in rough weather when you may have difficulty steering clear at the last minute.

You must also consider the possibility that an approaching large ship might be in the throes of avoiding collision with other ships that you cannot see over the horizon. She may not have seen you, and might suddenly alter course to avoid one of them and end up running into you.

In restricted waters you must also allow for the time and distance required by a large vessel to slow down or turn, the often limited visibility from the bridge, and the horrendous loss of control that could ensue if such a ship had to go full astern in an emergency.

◆ **Always take positive avoidance action in good time, well before there is any need for a large vessel to act. If you get too close a simple mistake could prove disastrous.**

◆ **A small vessel may be almost invisible in a seaway, and as a result she cannot rely on a big ship to steer clear according to the rules.**

You must consider whether you would be able to get clear of a passing vessel that suddenly ran amok with a mechanical breakdown, especially if you are under sail with no engine.

The lesson to be learned here is that it is bad policy to get so close to a large ship that there is real danger of collision. The rules basically lay down the required conduct of vessels at close quarters, so that they may avoid colliding with each other, but in a small boat you should whenever possible take avoidance action early enough to prevent such a situation developing. Whether you have 'right-of-way' or not, the problems involved in closing with a large ship should make you think twice about ever doing so if you can avoid it. But you must take such avoidance action (which may be very slight) long before there is the slightest possibility of the large ship doing the right thing by the rules, or you will make the situation far worse. The rules state quite clearly that if you do not have to give way, you should hold your course and speed – so that the other vessel knows what you are doing, and can thus take safe avoiding action. See Rule 17 (Chapter 12) for more on this very important aspect of interpreting the rules. Rule 2 (Chapter 1) is also relevant to this question.

1 DEFINITIONS

The first three rules basically 'set the scene' for the remainder by providing essential definitions and explanations. They are paraphrased in simple terms below.

Rule 1: Application

Rule 1(a) says in effect that the rules apply to all vessels on the high seas, and also in waters connected to them that are navigable by sea-going vessels. The definition of a sea-going vessel is not made, but presumably the inference is that they apply in harbours, up rivers and canals connected with the sea, and so on. Land-locked lakes, however, clearly escape this jurisdiction, so in such places very careful note must be made of local regulations.

Even in areas covered by the rules, special local regulations may be in force (particularly in large commercial harbours) and Rule 1(b) specifically allows for these local regulations to override the rules. It does, however, state that such regulations should conform as closely as possible to the rules. The U.S. Inland Navigation Rules (incorporating the Western Rivers Rules, Great Lakes Rules and earlier Inland Rules) are an example: written in 1980, they are in force inland throughout the large river systems and lakes of the United States.

Similar clearance is given by Rule 1(c) to special light and sound signals and shapes used by warships in convoy, or fishing boats working in fleets. These signals should be quite distinct, so that they cannot be confused with signals prescribed in Part D of the rules (Sound and Light Signals). Rule 1(d) simply says that traffic separation schemes may be enforced for the purpose of the rules (see Chapter 6).

Rule 1(e) allows certain vessels of unusual construction to depart from the permitted positioning of lights, foghorns and so on. The lights of a warship, for example, will often vary from the expected configuration owing to the positions of the masts or the shape of the vessel (see Chapter 23).

Rule 2: Responsibility

This fundamental rule states, in effect, that the rules shall not override commonsense and good seamanship when the safety of a vessel may be in danger. Rules are made for the guidance of wise men and the obedience of fools, and the Colregs are no exception. Rule 2, which should be firmly etched in the minds of all seamen, says that the responsibility for the vessel remains with the skipper at all times, and if the safety of his ship requires him to depart from the rules, then depart he must.

➡ Technically the rules require both ship A and the small motor cruiser to alter course to starboard to avoid each other. But the presence of ship B makes it more prudent for the small boat to alter to port, into water that is too shallow for the big ships.

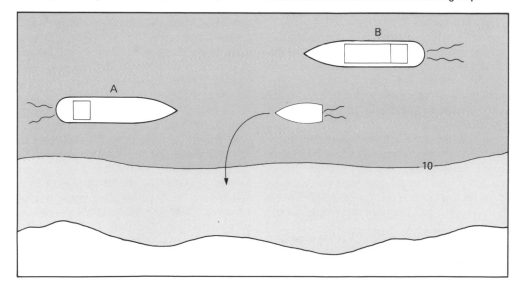

Rule 3: General definitions

Rule 3 lists the precise definitions of words and phrases used in the rules. Of particular importance are the following:

Underway means not attached to the ground (anchored, berthed, aground etc); it does *not* mean moving through the water.
Making way means moving through the water, and the distinction is important with respect to the lights shown by certain vessels.
Power-driven vessel includes sailing yachts that are motor-sailing.

➤ A yacht is only classed as a sailing vessel under the rules if she is under sail alone. When motor-sailing she is classed as a power-driven vessel.

Vessel
Any craft capable of being used on water; including seaplanes and hovercraft
Power-driven vessel
Any vessel propelled by machinery
Sailing vessel
Any vessel under sail, *so long as machinery is not being used*
Vessel engaged in fishing
Any vessel fishing with nets, lines, trawls etc that restrict her manoeuvrability; *does not include angling boats or fishing boats on passage*
Seaplane
Any aircraft designed to manoeuvre on the water
Vessel not under command
Any vessel unable to manoeuvre as required by the rules, so unable to keep clear of others
Vessel restricted in her ability to manoeuvre
A vessel that because of her work cannot manoeuvre to keep clear of others (see Chapter 12 for examples)
Vessel constrained by her draft
A power-driven vessel with such deep draft that she is constrained by the prevailing depth or width of water
In sight
Vessels are 'in sight' *only* when they can be observed *visually* from each other (*not* when on radar alone)
Restricted visibility
Any condition in which visibility is restricted by fog, rain, mist, falling snow, sandstorms etc.

In this book the following short terms will be used in place of the ones above:
Power vessel = power-driven vessel
Fishing vessel = vessel engaged in fishing
Not under command = vessel not under command
Restricted vessel = vessel restricted in her ability to manoeuvre
Constrained vessel = vessel constrained by her draft
Fog = restricted visibility

2 GENERAL CONDUCT

The steering and sailing rules which make up Part B of the Collision Regulations are divided into three sections. The rules in Section 1 cover general behaviour that will help vessels avoid situations where collision is possible. Section 2 covers specific manoeuvring for avoiding a collision between two vessels in sight of each other, and Section 3 covers action that should be taken in restricted visibility to prevent collisions.

Rules 4 to 10 are included in Section 1.

Rule 4: Application

This rule simply states that the rules in Section 1 apply in *any* condition of visibility.

Rule 5: Lookout

Rule 5 emphasises that vessels should keep a proper lookout at all times. This may seem rather obvious, but it does draw attention to both the variety of ways in which a lookout can be kept, and also the blind spots that can arise from weather conditions, human nature and so on.

The word 'lookout' is used in a very loose sense here. The actual rule states that it should be kept 'by sight and hearing as well as by all available means . . .' Eyes, ears, binoculars and radar are all means of keeping a lookout, each having its advantages and its limitations. Your eyes should be your first line of defence, and you should maintain a proper lookout routine, rather than just a glance around now and then. Many modern ships travel at great speed and the horizon viewed from the cockpit of a small yacht may be no more than three miles away, a distance that could be covered by a fast container ship in about ten minutes!

Your visual lookout should be constant: a steady sweep right round the horizon with your eyes, followed by the same with binoculars, then a few minutes to rest your eyes before repeating the exercise. Make sure you cover any blind arcs caused by sails, deckhouses or driving spray and rain, if necessary by briefly swinging the boat off course. At night it is important to realise that exposure to white light will ruin your night vision for nearly twenty minutes. Use dim red lights down below and reserve your flashlights, spotlights and spreader lights for emergencies.

In poor visibility you should maintain the same routine, but concentrate low down as a bow-wave is likely to be seen before a hull. In radiation fog try a lookout up the mast, as the fog is often very low-lying. You should also post lookouts forward and keep a listening watch at both ends of the boat if possible. If you are under power stop the engine periodically and have a good listen. By listening down below with an ear against the hull, you may detect propeller noise at a considerable distance and this will give you early warning of an approaching ship.

Keeping a radar watch is a specialised subject: see Chapter 14.

☞ Radiation fog is often low-lying, and a lookout up the mast will spot the superstructure of an approaching vessel long before the rest of the crew become aware of it.

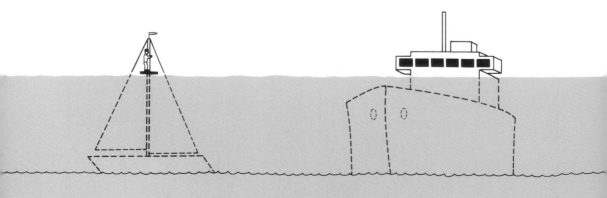

3 RISK OF COLLISION
Steering & Sailing Rules (Part B)

Rule 6: Safe speed

Rule 6 states that vessels should proceed at a safe speed. This means a speed sufficiently slow to enable you to take avoidance action in good time to prevent collision if another vessel suddenly appears at the limit of your visibility.

This statement is not quite as simple as it sounds. There are many reasons why a ship may suddenly appear at close range; they include fog, high seas, driving rain, and blinding shore lights, for example. There are also many things that can make a vessel slow to respond, even if she is actually moving relatively slowly: autopilots, spinnakers, boom preventers and seasick crews are just a selection. All these things must be taken into account when deciding on a safe speed. Another factor to bear in mind is traffic density. If there is a lot of shipping around it makes sense to proceed with caution.

When moving in fog using radar it is vital that you understand the capabilities and limitations of your equipment and operator. A naval vessel with a highly-trained and experienced technician operating a high-definition, narrow-beam minehunting radar can steam safely at a much greater speed than a yacht with an amateur peering now and then through salt-laden, red-rimmed and exhausted eyes at the tiny screen of a small instrument. (See Chapter 14).

Rule 7: Risk of collision

Rule 7 states that a vessel must use all available means to determine whether a risk of collision exists. For the small boat skipper this invariably means checking to see whether an approaching ship remains on a steady bearing. If this is the case, then the two of you will collide. If her bearing is drawing rapidly forward then she will pass ahead of you; if it draws aft she will pass astern.

Unless you maintain a very steady course, you should use a compass bearing rather than a relative bearing, for if you alter course and speed so the compass bearing on the other ship remains the same, you will still collide! However, if you are maintaining a steady course then a relative bearing will suffice, and it can be checked very simply by aligning the other vessel with a stanchion, mast or rigging and watching to see how she moves in relation to it. If she stays in line you will collide, and action should be taken according to Rules 11-18 (Section 2 of the Steering and Sailing Rules). Even if the bearing changes slowly there could still be a risk of collision, and Rule 7 specifically states that if you are in doubt, you must assume that there is a risk of collision.

➡ If boat A changes her course and speed the relative bearing of the converging vessel B will change too – but if its compass bearing remains constant, as here, they will still collide.

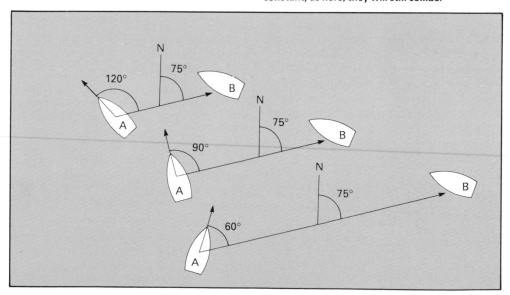

4 AVOIDING COLLISION

Rule 8: Action to avoid collision

This rule explains the general thinking that should lie behind any manoeuvre undertaken to avoid a collision. In principle it states that action should be taken early and boldly: early enough to prevent a close encounter with another vessel, and boldly enough for the other vessel to see exactly what you are doing, instantly. Most collisions occur because ships do not adhere to this simple, life-saving rule.

Rule 8 does not contradict the comments made in the Introduction regarding small vessels. The advice given there about slight alterations of course apply to removing the risk of collision long before it actually develops. If a risk of collision does develop, however, it is vital that the alteration of course is immediately obvious to the other vessel, to avoid the risk of her taking her own action according to Rule 2 (Chapter 1) or Rule 17 (Chapter 12).

So what constitutes a 'bold' alteration of course? The simple criterion is that your vessel should suddenly present a completely different aspect to the other, or at night a different coloured sidelight.

It is impossible to exaggerate the importance of Rule 8. Ships invariably collide because one vessel is uncertain of the other's intentions. If you are required to give way the initial priority is to show the other vessel three things: first that you have seen her; second that you intend giving way; and third what action you are going to take. All three are achieved very simply by an early, bold alteration of course – if necessary a far greater alteration than is required merely to avoid the collision. Having established your actions you can always haul steadily back towards your proper course.

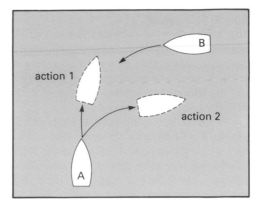

→ Boat A could try to avoid collision by simply slowing down and making a slight alteration of course (1), but this is unlikely to be apparent to B, who might panic and alter to port to go astern of A, increasing the chances of a collision. Boat A should make a bold course alteration (2), which leaves B in no doubt about what is happening.

A change of speed alone is rarely noticeable by the other vessel unless it is a rapid emergency stop by a fairly small boat. A drastic reduction in speed may, however, be useful at times to slow down the rate of closing. This could be combined with a bold alteration of course.

Whatever action you take you should always avoid crossing ahead of the other vessel if possible. In general, though, any alteration of course should be to starboard, as this is what the specific rules in Section 2 of the Steering and Sailing Rules invariably call for. This will extricate you from virtually all situations, as it will turn you away from any turn (to starboard) made by a closing vessel (see Chapters 10 and 11).

→ In a nearly head-on situation boat A should not be tempted to go to port. Boat B is very likely to alter to starboard, so A should do the same. (See Chapter 10).

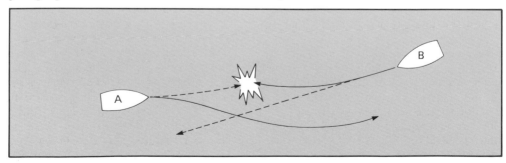

5 NARROW CHANNELS
Steering & Sailing Rules (Part B)

Rule 9: Narrow channels

There are a number of quite specific regulations included in this rule, but before considering them we need to decide just what is meant by a 'narrow channel'. The term is not actually defined in the rules. The reason, of course, is that the expression is relative to the size of the vessel: to a laden 500,000-ton tanker even the English Channel is narrow. In practice it should be quite obvious if a closing vessel is negotiating a channel that is narrow for her, and if doubt exists then this must be assumed.

The two main statements in Rule 9 are that vessels should keep to the starboard side of narrow channels, and that the progress of vessels confined to the channel must not be impeded by sailing boats, fishing boats or boats under 20 metres long. If you are in charge of such a boat you should take particular care when crossing a narrow channel, bearing in mind that a large vessel may be moving fast to maintain good steerage way. If you are in an engineless sailing vessel you need to take even more care, owing to the risk of getting becalmed in the channel, and you should certainly not anchor in the channel. It is important to realise that the large vessel is not holding her course simply because of the rules, but because she cannot deviate from it without running aground or causing mayhem in nearby moorings.

Overtaking in narrow channels is clearly fraught with risk, and this rule makes it plain that if the overtaken vessel has to take action to make room for the manoeuvre, then the vessel wanting to overtake *must* use the requisite sound signal (see Chapter 25). Having done so she is still subject to Rule 13 (Chapter 9).

Finally, vessels approaching a blind bend in a channel must navigate with great caution, and make the prescribed sound signal (see Chapter 25).

In most situations a small boat can simply remain in shallow water outside the main channel and thus avoid all problems. Canals, however, pose particular difficulties as this escape route is not available. It is important for a small boat to appreciate the dangers of the 'canal effect' caused by the pressure waves set up by a passing large vessel.

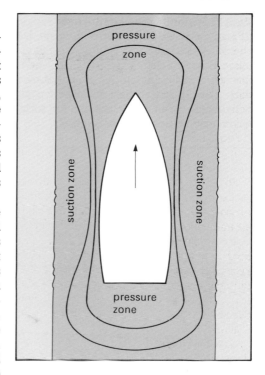

◆ In a canal the bow and stern waves cannot escape out sideways because of the closeness of the banks, so they are forced ahead and astern of the vessel, raising the water level and creating pressure zones as they go. Alongside the vessel the level falls to compensate, creating a suction zone. If the bow swings towards one bank the pressure zone can force it back in an uncontrolled sheer.

When approaching a large vessel head-on it is a mistake to give her a wide berth, partly because you risk grounding as the water is drawn from the banks as she passes, and partly because your bow may be pushed away from the bank by your own boat's pressure zone, causing you to swing towards her. You should pass her as closely as possible, for the pressure from her bow-wave will push you safely clear of her bow.

If you are being overtaken the situation is slightly different, as there is a greater risk of her amidships suction zone pulling you into her. You should reduce speed gently and move over towards the bank very gradually to avoid the risk of a sheer. Make use of the sound signals specified in Part D of the Collision Regulations (see Chapter 25).

6 TRAFFIC SEPARATION SCHEMES

Traffic separation schemes are in operation in many places where there is congested shipping, and they are clearly marked on charts. They provide one-way lanes in each direction, with a 'separation zone' between them. Usually there is also an 'inshore zone' between the main traffic lane and the coast, which may be used by small vessels.

◆ A typical traffic separation scheme, showing the one-way traffic lanes and separation zones. The inshore traffic zones near the coast are for small vessels that need to keep clear of heavy shipping.

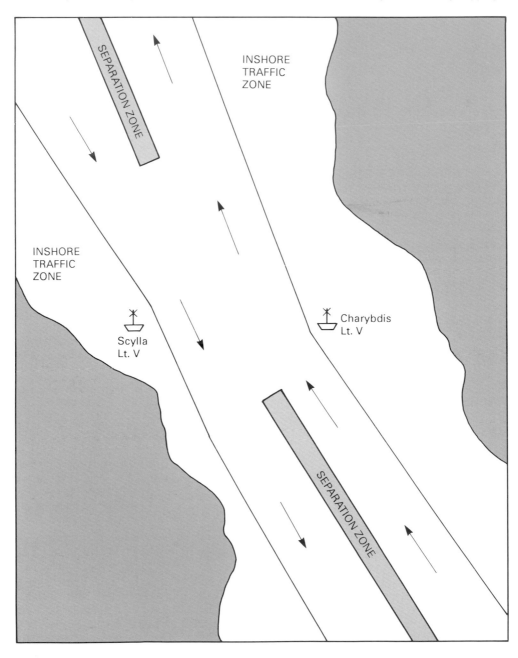

Rule 10: Traffic separation schemes

This rule is quite complex, but for the small boat skipper it boils down to the following:

1 Fishing boats, sailing boats and boats under 20 metres should not hinder the passage of vessels following a traffic lane.
2 Such boats should use inshore traffic zones rather than main traffic lanes.
3 No vessel should anchor in or near a traffic separation scheme.
4 Vessels should cross traffic lanes as rapidly as possible, and on a heading that is as close as possible to a right-angle with the heading of the traffic.
5 If, despite all these precautions, a risk of collision does arise with a vessel following a traffic lane, then the normal right-of-way rules in Section 2 will apply.

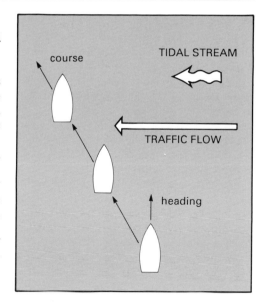

Number 5 is an interesting point. Although clearly it is intended to cope with unforeseen situations as well as general stupidity, it effectively permits an engineless sailing boat to create general mayhem within traffic lanes. It is extremely important that, if you are the skipper of such a vessel, you follow the spirit of this rule rather than the letter. You should make a very careful assessment of the prevailing situation before attempting to cross a traffic lane, especially in light winds, and you should try to do so in an area clear of surrounding navigational hazards and where the shipping in the lane is least concentrated. You should take care to avoid areas where vessels turn, or where

← The heading of the crossing vessel must be at right-angles to the traffic flow, regardless of her actual course which may be substantially affected by tidal streams.

they join and leave the scheme, owing to the difficulties caused by a concentration of shipping steaming in different directions. You would be well advised to avoid crossing at all during darkness, except perhaps in fresh and totally reliable winds, because of the uncertainty of being seen.

← With the tidal stream under her lee bow a sailing boat will point closer to the wind than when it is on her weather bow. This is very useful when beating across a traffic lane, since the boat's course is more nearly at right-angles to the traffic flow.

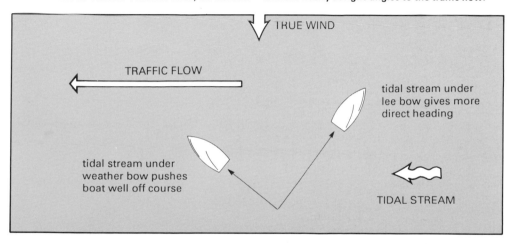

7 LIGHT AND COLLISION SECTORS

The next section of the rules governs conduct of vessels in sight of one another, and describes the specific actions to be taken when a risk of collision exists.

The first rule in the section, Rule 11, emphasises that the whole section applies to vessels *in sight* of one another. In other words, it does *not* apply when closing vessels can observe each other only on radar. They *must* be able to see each other with their eyes before applying Rules 12-18.

As there is a close relationship between the sectors over which navigation lights are displayed and the sectors governing collision avoidance, it will be helpful to consider these sectors together here.

All the relevant sectors are shown in the diagram, and the only thing you have to remember is that the cut-off line on either side is 22½° abaft the beam, or a quarter of the way from beam to stern. A green starboard sidelight shows from ahead round the starboard side to the cut-off line (GREEN IS RIGHT THESE DAYS). A red port sidelight covers the same arc on the port side (SAILORS DRINK RED PORT), and a white sternlight shows aft over the remaining arc.

The starboard sidelight covers the sector in which approaching vessels have right of way when two power-driven vessels meet. You must give way to vessels approaching you from anywhere in the sector covered by your green navigation light: hence the GREEN GIVE-WAY SECTOR. This assumes that the vessel is of a type you must give way to: see Chapter 12.

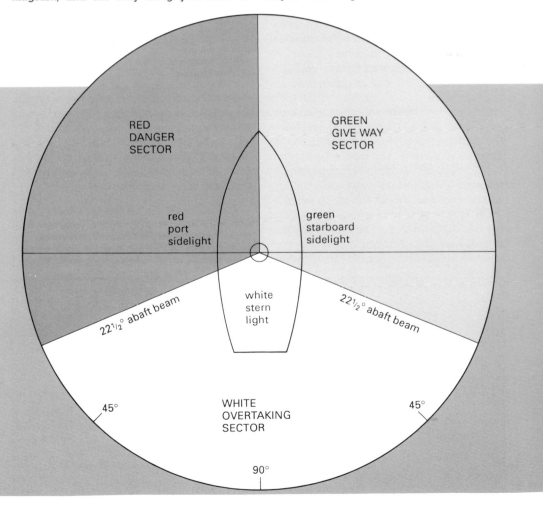

The RED FOR DANGER sector, covered by your port sidelight, signifies that vessels approaching you in this sector must give way to you, so they need to be watched with great care.

The sternlight is sometimes called the overtaking light as it shines over the OVERTAKING SECTOR, and an overtaking vessel is defined as one that approaches you within this arc. She must keep clear.

The reason for the relationship between light sectors and give-way sectors is, of course, that it makes it perfectly clear at night which of another vessel's sectors you lie in, and therefore which of you must give way. Most of the mnemonics in the next section are related to the colours of the sidelights.

Although these sectors refer to the red and green sidelights, in practice these lights are often not visible on large ships at the ranges at which you are likely to want to take action. Power-driven vessels, however, also display a more powerful white masthead light that shows over the combined arcs of the sidelights. Large vessels display two of these, the after one higher than the forward one. The relationship between these two masthead lights will indicate precisely which arc you are in, besides giving immediate warning of a course alteration (see Chapter 4). Virtually all collision avoidance of large ships should be done with the aid of these masthead lights, long before sidelights come within visibility range.

● It should be apparent that any alteration of course will make the masthead lights draw together or draw apart, depending on the aspect of the vessel and the way she is turning. The lights of a vessel beam-on will draw closer together whichever way she turns. If she is heading in your direction they will close up if she alters towards you, coming in line when she points directly at you. If she carries on turning they will open until she is beam-on, then steadily close again. Eventually they disappear when you bear 22½ degrees abaft her beam, to be replaced by the much lower sternlight.

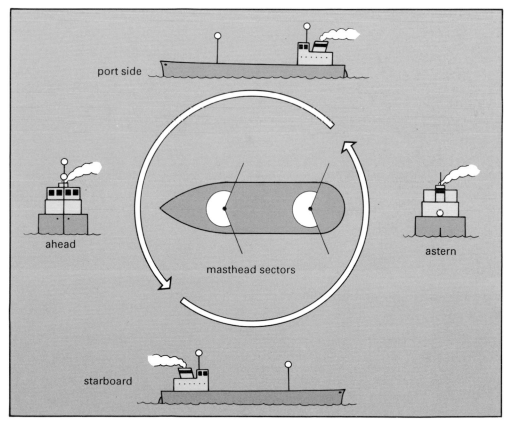

port side

ahead

masthead sectors

astern

starboard

8 SAILING VESSELS

Rule 12: Sailing vessels

This rule is quite simple and concise. It can be summed up as follows:

1 Port tack boat keeps clear (whatever the point of sailing)
2 Windward boat keeps clear (if both on same tack)
3 If in doubt about (1), keep clear

It can be remembered easily by the following rhyme:

> If on port or if in doubt
> Or if to windward – get on out

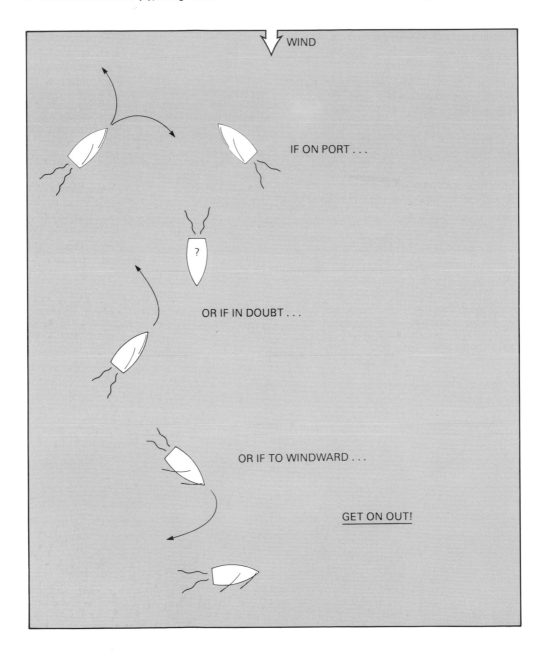

WIND

IF ON PORT . . .

?

OR IF IN DOUBT . . .

OR IF TO WINDWARD . . .

GET ON OUT!

The requirement for (3) becomes apparent when you are close-hauled on port tack at night, when it is often not possible to tell which tack a boat approaching from windward is on. The skipper must assume she is on starboard, and give way accordingly.

The windward side of a vessel is defined as the side opposite that on which the mainsail (or the largest fore-and-aft sail) is being carried. The tack that a vessel is sailing on is named after the windward side.

There are four situations that could create doubt under this rule:

1 Running under spinnaker alone (which side is the mainsail?)
2 Hove-to (which tack?)
3 During the tacking process (which tack?)
4 When a tack is needed in order to stand away from danger

In the first case common sense decrees that the windward side is that on which the spinnaker boom is set, for this is normally opposite the mainsail.

The second case should be determined by the position of the mainsail, or where it *would* be if it were set.

The racing fraternity have a rule to cover the third situation, but to a vessel at sea it should be plainly obvious that another in the throes of tacking (especially a large one with complex rig) is not fully under command and should be given a wide berth (see Chapter 12). At close quarters the tacking boat can hail the other and warn her of the manoeuvre.

The same solution can be adopted when you have to put in a tack to clear a danger, such as shallow water. At ranges beyond hailing distance you should have time to complete the tack and get going again before you meet the other vessel. If you are the other vessel you will be able to tell from your chart that such a tack is about to take place, and you should avoid cramping the other as she sails clear on the new tack. You will need to apply flexibility, common sense, good seamanship and courtesy when large numbers of yachts are tacking up a narrow river. You must look a long way ahead to foresee what others are likely to do.

Although it is officially considered unsporting to run on starboard tack purely to avoid having to give way, it is very commonly done – especially when under spinnaker or other sails that make manoeuvring difficult. When beating on port tack you should watch boats that are running down from windward on port tack, because they may gybe onto starboard at the last minute to avoid having to give way.

→ Boat A, running before the wind under spinnaker alone, is on port tack because the spinnaker pole is set on the port (windward) side. Boat B is hove-to on starboard tack – a wise precaution since other boats have to keep clear.

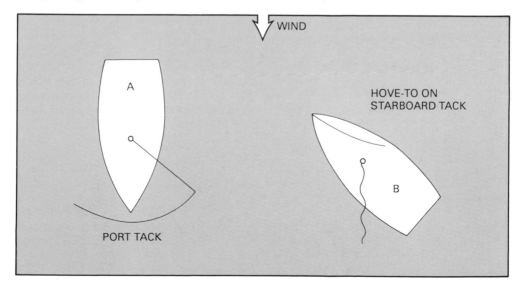

9 OVERTAKING VESSELS

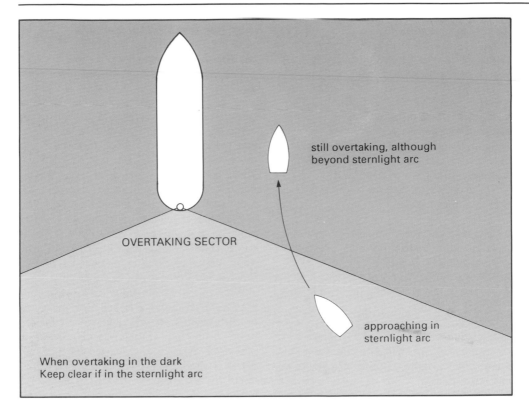

still overtaking, although
beyond sternlight arc

OVERTAKING SECTOR

approaching in
sternlight arc

When overtaking in the dark
Keep clear if in the sternlight arc

Rule 13: Overtaking vessels

The rule states that *any vessel* must keep clear of another vessel that she is overtaking.

Any vessel means what it says: whether you are overtaking in a sailing boat, fishing boat or whatever, you must keep clear regardless of the type of vessel being overtaken. The logic behind this rule should be clear: the faster vessel keeps clear of the slower one.

An overtaking vessel is defined as one approaching in the overtaking arc (see Chapter 7), when (if it is dark) the only light she can see on the other vessel is the sternlight. Furthermore, she remains the overtaking vessel even after she has passed from this arc into that of a sidelight.

If you are in doubt as to whether you are in this arc, you must assume that you are and keep clear accordingly.

If you are the vessel being overtaken, and you are in doubt about the position of the other boat, then a sensible move might be to alter course (in good time) to place the other directly astern and definitely in the

◄ A boat approaching another in the arc of her sternlight is defined as an overtaking vessel, and must keep clear – even when she is passing abeam.

overtaking arc. This has the added benefit of bringing the courses nearly parallel, with you moving away from her track, so reducing greatly the risk of collision if the overtaking vessel makes no attempt to keep clear. If a serious risk of collision then develops, this action will have both reduced the closing speed and increased your options for escaping from danger, as you can see in the diagram opposite. This is perhaps one situation in which an alteration of course to port would be sound, on the assumption that a last-minute alteration by the overtaking vessel would be instinctively to starboard.

All these actions should be taken so as to avoid crossing ahead of the other vessel, and also long before there is a possibility of her manoeuvring to avoid you. Make the alteration (if you think it necessary) then stick to a steady course and speed so that the other knows what you are doing (assuming that you have been seen).

At this point it is worth emphasising the importance of checking astern before making *any* alteration of course, so that you do not suddenly alter course ahead of an overtaking vessel. Remember that such a vessel may appear from over the horizon very rapidly.

◆ By day the limits of the overtaking sector are not obvious, but if in doubt the overtaking vessel should assume she is in the sector and keep clear.

◆ In a doubtful overtaking situation the vessel being overtaken can alter course to place the other directly astern, then alter course again to avoid collision if necessary.

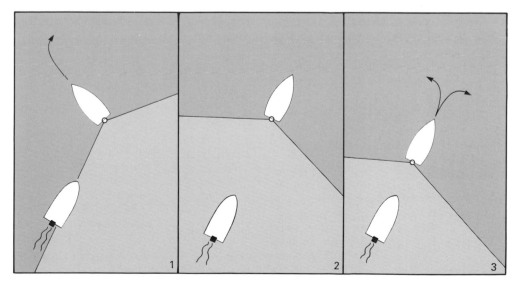

10 POWER VESSELS HEAD-ON

Rule 14: Head-on situation

The essence of this rule is that power vessels approaching head-on should alter course to starboard, and pass down each other's port side.

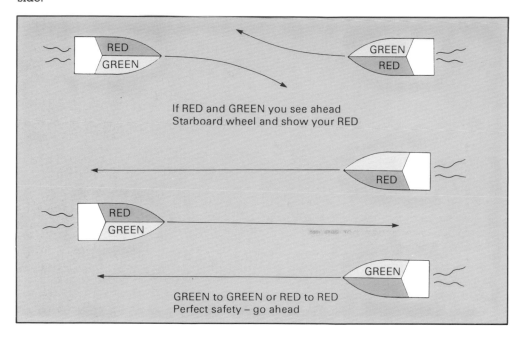

If RED and GREEN you see ahead
Starboard wheel and show your RED

GREEN to GREEN or RED to RED
Perfect safety – go ahead

This seems a very straightforward rule, yet it probably causes more trouble than any other. Problems arise when vessels approach *almost* head-on, steaming on reciprocal (or nearly reciprocal) courses that will pass very close, as shown below. There is a temptation here for boat A to make a slight alteration to port, to pull further away from the track of boat B so that they pass well clear down each other's starboard side. If this is done very early indeed, so that it is obvious that both vessels will pass well clear of each other, then there will be no problem. But if A leaves it a bit late, then

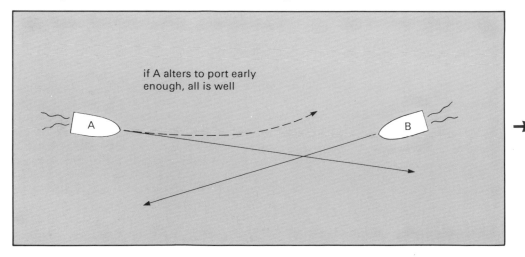

if A alters to port early enough, all is well

B might decide that a risk of collision exists and she must take avoiding action. She will alter course to starboard as required by the rules, confusion will set in as the two vessels swing towards each other, as in the diagram below, and the result could well be a collision. Boat A should foresee the likelihood of B altering to starboard and go boldly to starboard herself, so that the other can see exactly what she is doing.

The safest course of action by B if this situation develops is probably to stop, while A gets clear. If she continues turning to starboard, A may simply turn harder to port; if she alters back to port, A may panic and alter back to starboard. Either action will probably end in a collision.

Exactly the same problem can occur if A thinks as before, but B decides that A is on her starboard side and alters to starboard intending to pass under her stern (see Chapter 11). The rules allow for this possibility by saying that if doubt exists as to whether a head-on situation or a 'crossing situation' prevails, then the vessels must assume the former and both alter to starboard. It is rarely safe to alter to port in any closing situation, for these reasons. See Chapter 11 for further discussion of crossing situations.

This sort of collision is particularly common when vessels have each other on radar only, as it is then very difficult indeed to judge the aspect of the other ship, and thus the precise nature of the closing situation.

→ If approaching head-on, you should always alter course to starboard, as any other course of action will probably cause confusion and a collision.

→ The temptation to turn to port should be resisted, since the other vessel may turn to starboard – with catastrophic results.

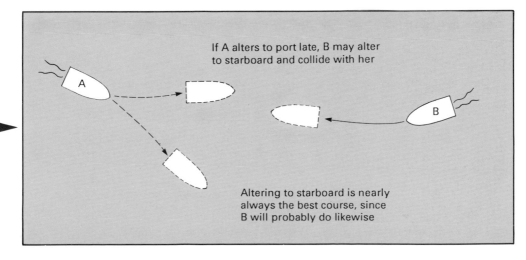

If A alters to port late, B may alter to starboard and collide with her

Altering to starboard is nearly always the best course, since B will probably do likewise

11 POWER VESSELS CROSSING

Rule 15: Crossing situation

Rule 15 states that the vessel with the other on its starboard side shall keep clear. The starboard side is the GREEN GIVE-WAY sector of the starboard sidelight (see Chapter 7).

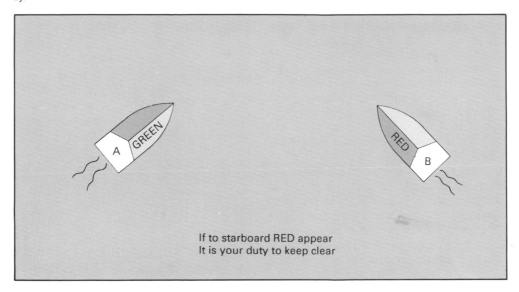

If to starboard RED appear
It is your duty to keep clear

Unless there is extremely good reason why you cannot do so, if you are in this position you should alter to starboard and pass under the other's stern (see below). The rules say that you 'should avoid crossing ahead', and it is dangerous seamanship to cross another vessel's bows at close quarters. If you have to make an alteration to port (perhaps because of the presence of other ships or navigational dangers) you should do it in very good time so as to pass well ahead, or continue the turn in a full circle while the other vessel goes clear. Alternatively you could slow right down to allow the other vessel clear passage ahead of you.

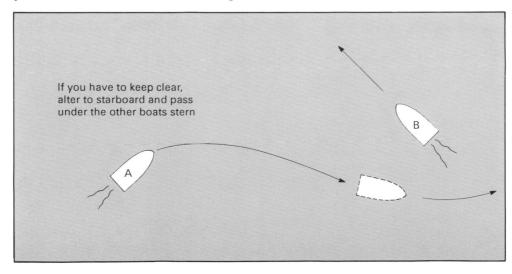

If you have to keep clear,
alter to starboard and pass
under the other boats stern

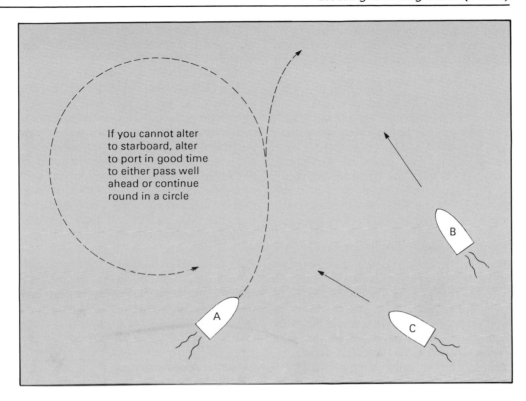

If you cannot alter to starboard, alter to port in good time to either pass well ahead or continue round in a circle

If you consider this rule together with the previous one, you can see that the normal action of a give-way vessel should be an alteration of course to starboard. In cases of doubt or difficult interpretation this action will almost certainly keep you out of trouble, assuming the other vessel does the same. Whatever the legalities of the situation, if both vessels turn to starboard they will at least swing away from each other. They will also know that each is certain to maintain that swing to starboard. As explained in Chapter 10, this is not the case if one vessel tries to be clever and alters to port.

If there is any doubt as to whether a crossing situation or a head-on situation prevails, the latter must be assumed and action taken by both vessels accordingly (see Chapter 10).

If doubt exists as to whether the other vessel is in your green sector or your overtaking sector the onus is on her to assume the latter (see Chapter 9). You must maintain a careful watch on the other vessel in such a situation in case the doubt you feel is not felt by her. This is one situation in which an alteration to port may be better than an alteration to starboard: see Chapter 9. It might be better to slow right down and let her pass clear ahead. Each situation must be judged on its merits at the time.

● If boat A is in B's overtaking sector, B should stand on while A keeps clear. If in doubt, A should keep clear anyway.

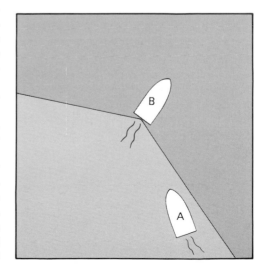

12 GENERAL RESPONSIBILITIES

Rule 16: Action by give-way vessel
The give-way vessel must take early and substantial action to keep clear. See Chapter 4.

Rule 17: Action by stand-on vessel
There are two important aspects to this rule. The first is that the stand-on vessel *must* hold her course and speed, so that the other can calculate her projected movement. Clearly if she starts altering course and speed as the vessels draw closer to each other, this could cause considerable confusion over who must keep clear, and how they can safely do so. See Chapter 9.

The second part of the rule, however, says that if it becomes apparent that the other vessel is not going to give way, the stand-on vessel *may* take such action as is necessary to avoid a collision. It also says that if a collision is inevitable unless action is taken by both vessels, the stand-on vessel *shall* take action to avoid it. The latter is a definite instruction for an emergency situation; the former permits the stand-on vessel some leeway in deciding when the point of no return is approaching, and allows her to take action before it arrives.

➡ If the stand-on vessel (B) alters to port instead of maintaining her course, the give-way vessel (A) may simultaneously alter to starboard according to the rules, leading to a collision. If B is in doubt about A's action she should turn away to starboard.

The significance of this to the small boat skipper lies in the first part, permitting him to take early action to keep clear of a large vessel that may not have seen him. However, he must always bear in mind the possibility that the other vessel may well have seen him, but is simply delaying the moment of taking action. This possibility must always be considered by the stand-on vessel, and any action taken by the latter must avoid the risk of the two vessels turning towards each other (see Chapters 9, 10 and 11). If in doubt the best action is probably to turn right away from the other vessel and show her your sternlight (see Chapter 9).

Rule 18: Responsibilities between vessels
What this rule boils down to is that a type of vessel in the boxed list opposite must give way to any other type that is higher in the list, unless Rules 9, 10 or 13 apply (see Chapters 5, 6 and 9). The logic is simple: the more manoeuvrable vessels keep clear of the less manoeuvrable ones.

Technically, a seaplane is obliged only to 'in general, keep well clear of all vessels and avoid impeding their navigation'. If a risk of collision does develop then she is to be treated as a power-driven vessel according to the rules.

A vessel constrained by her draft is treated rather hesitantly by this rule, which simply says that vessels below it on this list 'shall, if the circumstances of the case admit, avoid impeding the safe passage of a vessel constrained by her draft'. Since vessels

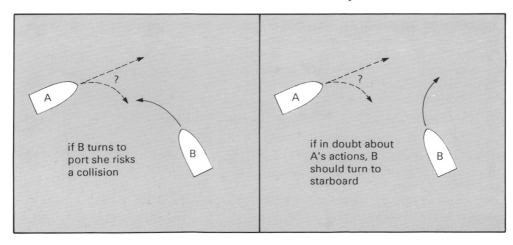

if B turns to port she risks a collision

if in doubt about A's actions, B should turn to starboard

Description of vessel	Shorthand	Mnemonic
Vessel not under command	NUC	Nuclear
Vessel restricted in her ability to manoeuvre	RESTRICTED	Restrictions
Vessel constrained by her draft	CONSTRAINED	Constrain
Vessel engaged in fishing	FISHING	Fishing (and)
Sailing vessel underway	SAILING	Sailing
Power-driven vessel underway	POWER	People
Seaplane	SEAPLANE	Say

below it on the list are *not* constrained by their draft, they can usually keep clear without difficulty, and this certainly applies to most small boats.

Note that a tug with a vessel in tow has no special rights by these rules unless the tow is particularly unwieldy, in which case she displays the lights or shapes for a vessel restricted in her ability to manoeuvre, in addition to the towing lights (see Chapters 18, 21). However, it would be discourteous in the extreme for a small sailing boat to stand on her rights when meeting a tow. Early, conspicuous action should be taken to keep clear.

Fishing vessels need to be given a wide berth, as they are liable to make sudden and unexpected alterations of course and speed, and may even steam round in circles. It is not wise to try threading a way through a fleet of fishing vessels showing red over white lights (see Chapter 20), because there will probably be long nets floating about close to the surface.

Restricted vessels

Vessels that may be restricted in their ability to manoeuvre include the following:

• Vessels handling navigation marks, submarine cables or pipelines.
• Vessels engaged in dredging, surveying or underwater operations.
• Vessels engaged in replenishment or transferring people or cargo while underway.
• Vessels launching or recovering aircraft.
• Vessels engaged in mine-clearance operations.
• Vessels engaged in towing operations that severely restrict their movements.

➥ **A large vessel constrained by her draft is easily avoided by keeping to shallow water.**

13 RESTRICTED VISIBILITY

Section 3 of the Steering and Sailing Rules applies to vessels *not* in sight of one another, owing to poor visibility. This can be caused not only by fog, but also by rain, snow and spray.

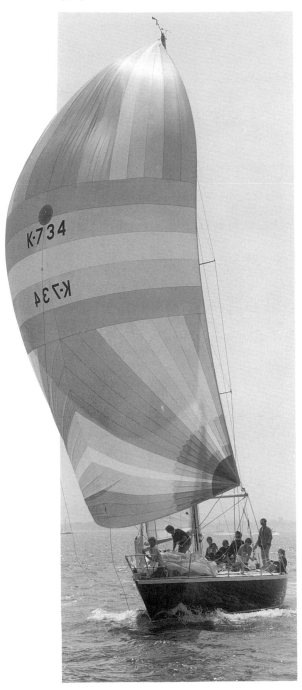

Rule 19: Conduct of vessels in restricted visibility

This rule lists the general precautions to be taken to reduce the risk of collision.

The first of these is that vessels should proceed at a safe speed and always be ready for rapid manoeuvring.

A 'safe speed' means a speed that enables avoiding action to be taken on sighting another vessel. For a small boat relying on eyesight this may mean 5 or 6 knots or even less, but bear in mind that a large ship with accurate radar and experienced operators may consider 30 knots to be perfectly safe.

The rules only refer to powerboats having engines ready for immediate manoeuvre, but the principle should also be applied to the rig of a sailing vessel. Spinnakers, boom preventers and suchlike should not be used in poor visibility, for obvious reasons. In calms, an auxiliary engine should be kept at instant readiness, by running it up occasionally to keep it warm. The importance of listening out for approaching vessels was discussed in Chapter 2, and if possible a sailing boat is best kept under sail to improve hearing – although the engine should be used to get clear of danger areas, such as shipping lanes, as quickly as possible.

Clause (d) of Rule 19 says that, unless you are certain that risk of collision does not exist, if you hear a fog signal forward of the beam you should reduce speed to no more than steerage way, and even stop if in doubt as to what is happening. You should then continue with extreme caution.

This rule makes a great deal of sense for large vessels. However, for a small boat that may not be visible on an approaching vessel's radar, or on that of a rapidly over-taking vessel, stopping could be a dangerous option. Except in the case of a high-speed powerboat which could quickly accelerate out of trouble, stopping could considerably reduce the boat's ability to take rapid evasive action.

◆ Setting a spinnaker in poor visibility is a mistake, since it will make the boat hard to handle if rapid avoidance action is necessary.

Another clause says that if you detect a possible close-quarters situation on radar you should, if taking avoiding action, refrain from altering course to port for a vessel forward of the beam, unless overtaking it. You should also avoid altering course towards a vessel abeam or abaft the beam. The reasons for these provisos should by now be apparent. See Chapters 2, 3, 4, 9 10 and 11. The diagram below shows two possible scenarios indicating the dangers inherent in either of these actions.

Apart from noting these particular rules the best course of action for a small boat in poor visibility is to hoist a good radar reflector (which will make the boat much easier to detect) and head into shallow water where large ships cannot go. Traffic lanes and other areas of shipping concentrations should be vacated as rapidly as possible. Use the appropriate sound signal for your vessel, and learn the meanings of other sound signals (see Chapter 25).

➤ **The traditional octahedral radar reflector, mounted in the correct 'catch-rain' position (left), and a modern encapsulated model (right).**

➤ **Since the radar screen gives no indication of aspect, mistakes are easily made.**

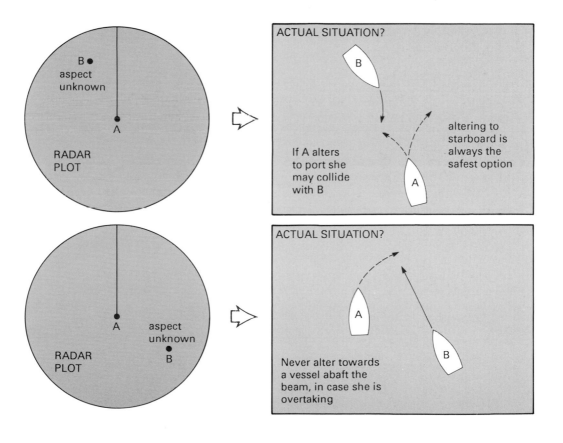

14 RADAR AND RADIO

Radar is an extremely useful anti-collision aid, especially in poor visibility. As with any tool, you need to know how it works to get the best out of it. Unfortunately, unlike most other tools, this one can cause the most horrendous destruction and loss of life if it is not used properly.

The well-known saying 'radar-assisted collision' is not a joke, but an all-too-frequent fact. It is caused, by and large, by one or more radar operators misinterpreting the information displayed on their screens. Collisions can also be caused by operators incorrectly setting up and tuning their sets, so that small or weak echoes, such as yachts, simply do not show at all. In certain conditions such echoes may not show however well the set is tuned. Radar is a useful aid, but it is not infallible. You must keep a visual watch as well.

For a small vessel, radar provides valuable early warning of other vessels in the vicinity, but you should be very wary of using it for collision avoidance at close quarters. You need professional training to do so safely, and even with training a small boat radar will have neither the accuracy nor the 'height of eye' (to give it a good enough range) for such potentially dangerous operations.

The main problem is assessing the aspect of the other vessel. Radar gives no direct indication of this, and unless you know it, you cannot decide on appropriate avoiding action. The diagrams opposite show the type of confusion that can arise. If at all possible, it is best to rely on your eyes when manoeuvring at close quarters.

Reliance on the other ship's radar

It is equally dangerous to rely on being detected by the radar of the other ship, for a number of very good reasons. Even when equipped with a good radar reflector a small boat presents a very poor target at the best of times, and in rough weather her echo can be masked by echoes from waves (known as 'sea clutter'). Small-boat echoes also tend to be intermittent, because the boat bobs up and down behind waves. As a result the Officer of the Watch, glancing now and then at the display, may never actually see them. The slightest mis-tuning of the set will wipe them out anyway, as will rain squalls.

Even in perfect conditions, with a good echo steadily displayed on the ship's screen, trouble can arise all too easily because of the relative motion of the picture. The ship is in the centre of the screen and the movement of echoes is relative to that of the ship; there is no indication of the heading, course or speed of targets. These things have to be calculated. The sort of problem described in Chapter 10 (slight alteration to port in a head-on situation) is even more dangerous when relying on radar than it is when vessels are in sight, for the result of an incorrect avoidance action to port takes some time to show on the screen. It can be very difficult to assess what is happening in such a situation, and many ships have collided for precisely this reason.

→ A radar set with a theoretical range of 48 miles may see only 5–10 miles to the horizon, plus a little more for the height of the target ship.

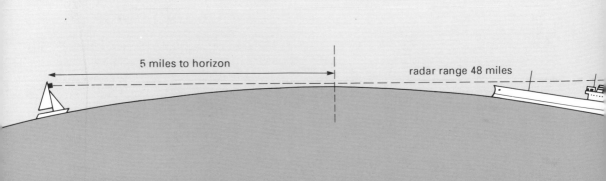

5 miles to horizon   radar range 48 miles

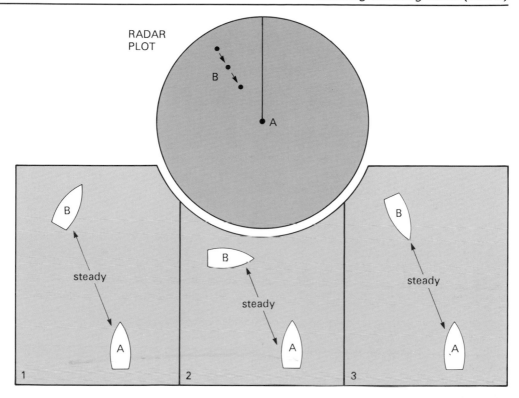

◄ The target B moves down the screen towards you on a steady relative bearing. Your course and speed are steady, so a risk of collision exists. What action do you take? This relative closing effect could be caused by any of the three situations depicted. In situation 1 you are overtaking the target, and must give way. In situation 2 you are in the green sector of the target, and must hold your course and speed. In situation 3 you are approaching virtually head-on, so both vessels must alter course to starboard. The potential problems faced by an inexperienced operator should be obvious.

VHF radio

VHF radio can help prevent collisions in certain circumstances. When you are approaching areas controlled by radar and radio, such as large commercial harbours and bottlenecks like the Strait of Gibraltar, you can learn a great deal about the movement of shipping by listening in to the control channel. Not only will you gain information about the position, course and speed of approaching ships, but you will also get warning of impending course alterations as two big ships prepare to avoid each other. This is useful, because these avoidance actions by large

vessels may not be what you are expecting. For example, alterations to port in a head-on situation may be arranged by the vessels concerned, in collusion with the harbour control, to avoid navigational difficulties or risk of collision with other vessels.

Another way in which VHF can help is by clarifying the actions of an approaching vessel; will she shortly be altering course towards a nearby harbour, for example, thus cutting across your intended track? Bear in mind that she may not have seen you. Such vessels may be contacted on Channel 16 by a call such as: 'Large black tanker four miles off Berry Head, this is . . .'

This should not, however, become a routine method of collision avoidance, for three good reasons. The first is the uncertainty of contacting the vessel; the second is the possibility of discussing things with the wrong ship; the third is that excessive use of the radio will clutter up the already busy airwaves. The whole point of the Collision Regulations is to enable vessels to avoid collision without having recourse to a radio conversation.

15 LIGHTS: GENERAL DEFINITIONS

Rule 20: Application
Rule 20 lists a number of general instructions regarding lights and shapes. These include the following:

- Rules in this section must be applied in all weathers.
- Lights shall be exhibited from sunset to sunrise.
- Lights shall also be exhibited when necessary (as in poor visibility).
- No extra lights should interfere or be confused with these lights.
- No lighting should affect the lookout.
- Shapes shall be exhibited during the day.

Rule 21: Definitions
The various lights are defined under this rule. The masthead light, sternlight and sidelights were described in Chapter 7, and the others are as follows:

Towing light = a yellow version of the sternlight
All-around light = a light which shows over an arc of 360°
Flashing light = a light which flashes at 120 flashes per minute (minimum)

Rule 22: Visibility of lights
The prescribed intensities of lights vary according to the length of the vessel. The method of determining the actual power of each light is covered in Annex 1 of the rules, but the practical minimum visibilities for various sizes of vessel should be as follows:

Light	Length of vessel	Visibility (miles)
Masthead	under 12 m	2
	12-20 m	3
	20-50 m	5
	over 50	6
Side	under 12 m	1
	12-50 m	2
	over 50 m	3
Stern	under 50 m	2
	over 50 m	3

The visibility of towing and all-around lights should be the same as that of the sternlight. All-around white lights on semi-submerged towed objects should have a visibility of three miles.

The length of a tow is defined in the rule covering lights for towing vessels, but it is convenient to note here that a tow is measured from the stern of the towing vessel to the after end of the tow.

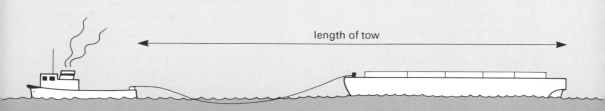

➤ The length of a tow includes the vessel being towed, as well as the cable.

length of tow

16 INTERPRETING LIGHTS AND SHAPES

The lights shown by vessels at sea can be extremely complex at times. Certain types of dredger, for example, show 12 different lights, all of them significant. Any attempt to remember every single light shown by every single type of vessel under all circumstances is almost certainly doomed to failure.

However, on close examination a pattern emerges. Most lights occur in clearly-defined groupings, each group of lights representing a certain activity that may be common to a number of different vessels. So rather than attempt to memorise a long list of lights for each vessel, you can memorise the lights forming each group, and the activity represented by that group. Each vessel can then be considered in terms of her activities, and therefore the groups of lights she will display.

To reduce the number of words to remember for each vessel the following concise notation is employed in descriptions:

Steaming = masthead light (as it is shown only by power vessels)
Aft steaming = second masthead light abaft and higher than steaming
Tow steaming = second masthead light vertically above steaming
WHITE; RED = all-around light of stated colour
Bow lantern = single lamp, normally at bow, containing both sidelights
Mast lantern = same at masthead containing sidelights and sternlight

The use of the term steaming light in preference to masthead light is very common in practice. It is deliberately used here as a useful reminder that masthead lights are shown only by vessels under power. Tow steaming lights are shown by tugs, and this name also serves as a reminder.

All-around lights indicate the function of a vessel (a fishing or pilot boat, for example) and are always grouped vertically. They can be simply described in the form RED over WHITE, etc.

Bow and mast lanterns are commonly used in sailing vessels as they provide two or three lights from one bulb, thus saving valuable electricity. (In order to maintain a sharp cut-off point between the lights these lanterns must have vertical filament bulbs.)

It should be clearly understood that a mast lantern is an *alternative* to normal navigation lights, not an addition. The all-too-frequent display of both (to make the yacht more visible?) serves only to confuse (see Chapter 24).

Steaming lights should be noticeably higher than all others, although in practice all-around 'function' lights may be close beneath them (some may in fact be above – see Chapters 21 and 22). To comply with this requirement, a yacht with a mast lantern must *never* use it with a steaming light when motoring. Considerable confusion can be caused by this common malpractice (see Chapter 24). A yacht should carry additional conventional navigation lights well below the steaming light, and use them when motoring. See Chapter 19 for details of the lights to be carried by yachts.

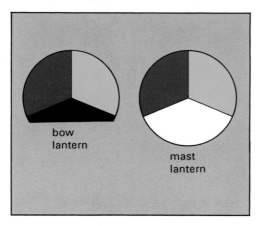

bow
lantern

mast
lantern

To further condense and simplify the presentation of lights the following symbols will be used:

FL = flashing light (120 flashes/minute minimum)
Making way = when vessel is moving through the water
Underway = when vessel is not attached to the ground

Groupings of lights will be indicated as follows:
Navigation = sidelights and sternlight
Power = lights shown by powered vessel (according to size)
Anchor = lights shown by anchored vessel (according to size)
NUC = RED over RED (Not Under Command)
Restricted = RED over WHITE over RED

Navigation lights (with certain logical exceptions) show that a vessel is underway.

NUC lights show that a vessel is not under command: she may have a steering breakdown, for example. They are used in a number of related situations.

Restricted lights show that a vessel is restricted in her ability to manoeuvre. These lights are shown by a variety of vessels: see Chapter 12.

Certain shapes are also shown by many different vessels and the following concise terms will be used:

Anchor ball = BLACK BALL forward (denotes vessel anchored)
Restricted = BLACK BALL over BLACK DIAMOND over BLACK BALL

In the following pages you will find the various types of vessel listed with details of the lights and shapes carried, a selection of pictures of the lights as seen from various angles, and some comments and mnemonics to help you remember them. The vessels are grouped as in the Collision Regulations, in the order in which they occur there.

The angles of view of the lights are deliberately varied, for two reasons. Firstly to aid identification from the angles that provide most difference in the light clusters, and secondly to encourage a flexible approach to identification.

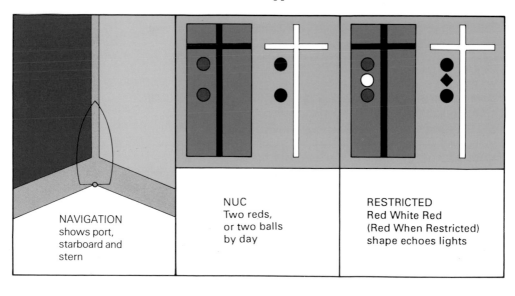

NAVIGATION
shows port,
starboard and
stern

NUC
Two reds,
or two balls
by day

RESTRICTED
Red White Red
(Red When Restricted)
shape echoes lights

17 POWER-DRIVEN VESSELS (Rule 23)

Type of vessel	Lights shown
VESSEL UNDER POWER	☆ navigation ☆ steaming ☆ aft steaming (optional less than 50 m) Shape = NONE
Less than 20 m	☆ power (as above) OR ☆ steaming + stern + bow lantern Shape = NONE
Less than 12 m	☆ power OR ☆ WHITE + sidelights/bow lantern Shape = NONE
Less than 7 m; Less than 7 knots	☆ power OR ☆ WHITE + sidelights/bow lantern (optional)
HOVERCRAFT; some SUBMARINES	☆ power ☆ FLASHING YELLOW (hovering) Shape = NONE
LIFEBOAT; FIRING RANGE BOAT; CUSTOMS BOAT; POLICE BOAT	☆ power ☆ FLASHING BLUE Shape = NONE
VESSEL CARRYING EXPLOSIVES	☆ power ☆ RED Shape = Code FLAG B

Views			Memory aids and comments
side-on	stern-on	bow-on	
over 50m			UNDERWAY so shows NAVIGATION lights. UNDER POWER so shows STEAMING lights. TOO LONG a vessel shows TWO WHITE STEAMING lights.
			As above. 2-mile range (or 1-mile range) sidelights may be combined as 1 bow lantern (see Chapter 15)
			As above. 2-mile steaming light may be combined with sternlight as 1 WHITE (see Chapter 15)
			As above. Under SEVEN metre has SINGLE light (WHITE). May show sidelights/bow lantern as well
			Being POWER-driven she shows POWER lights. FLASHING YELLOW = WARNING: things are not what they seem; one ship flies above the water; the other sinks beneath it. The slower submarine has a slower FLASHING YELLOW; 90-105 per min against 120 per min
			Being POWER-driven she shows POWER lights. FLASHING BLUE like emergency services ashore
			Being POWER-driven she shows POWER lights. RED for DANGEROUS cargo. See International Code

36

18 TOWING AND PUSHING (Rule 24)

Vessel	Lights shown
VESSEL TOWING (or towing alongside) (or pushing)	☆ power ☆ tow steaming ☆ towing Shape = NONE
VESSEL TOWING Length of tow more than 200 m	☆ as above ☆ 2nd tow steaming above 1st Shape = DIAMOND ◆
VESSEL BEING TOWED	☆ navigation Shape = DIAMOND ◆ (tow more than 200 m)
VESSEL BEING PUSHED	☆ sidelights forward ☆ sternlight (if alongside tug)
SEMI-SUBMERGED TOW	☆ WHITE aft ☆ WHITE forward (except dracones) Shape = DIAMOND aft + DIAMOND forward (tow more than 200 m) ◆ ◆
Towed object more than 25 m wide	☆ as above ☆ WHITE on each beam Shape = as above
Towed object more than 100 m long	☆ as semi-submerged tow ☆ extra WHITES so no lights more than 100 m apart Shape = as above
COMPOSITE TUG & TOW	☆ power
VESSEL TOWING, with no proper towing lights	☆ all possible means to indicate tow, such as searchlight illuminating towline etc

Views			Memory aids and comments
side-on	stern-on	bow-on	
under 50m		over 50m	Being POWER-driven, shows POWER lights. SECOND STEAMING light indicates SECOND SHIP in tow. YELLOW towing light WARNS – overtaking arc not clear
			Standard TOWING lights for TOWING vessel. TWO TOW steaming lights indicate TWO hundred metre TOW. Big tow shows expensive shape (DIAMOND)
			Being UNDERWAY, shows NAVIGATION lights. NOT STEAMING, so NO STEAMING lights. Shape mirrors tug shape
starboard bow	alongside	alongside	UNDERWAY so NAVIGATION lights, forward where visible. Sternlight shows total width when tow alongside
			WHITES at each end show presence and extent of object. Dracone submerged forward so cannot show forward light
			WHITES on each beam show extent of very wide object
			WHITES spread along the length to deter passage through middle of very long object; compare with decklights on long anchored vessel
			Treated as a single vessel
			See Rule 36 in Chapter 25. Other vessels must be alerted to presence of tow

19 SAILING AND ROWING (Rule 25)

Vessel	Lights shown
VESSEL UNDER SAIL	☆ navigation ☆ RED over GREEN (optional) Shape = NONE
Less than 20 m	☆ as above OR ☆ mast lantern Shape = NONE
Less than 7m or under oars	☆ navigation OR ☆ mast lantern OR ☆ WHITE in time to prevent collision Shape = None
VESSEL MOTOR-SAILING	☆ power Shape = CONE (point down) forward. ▼ DO NOT USE MAST LANTERN WITH STEAMING LIGHT

LIGHTS FITTED TO YACHTS TO COVER SAILING AND MOTORING

Vessel	Lights fitted	Views
		motoring
More than 20 m	☆ steaming light ☆ sidelights ☆ sternlight ☆ anchor light (WHITE)	
Less than 20 m	☆ steaming light ☆ sidelights OR bow lantern ☆ sternlight ☆ mast lantern (optional) ☆ anchor light	
Less than 12 m	☆ sidelights OR bow lantern ☆ WHITE (can double as anchor light) ☆ sternlight ☆ mast lantern (optional)	

Views			Memory aids and comments
side-on	stern-on	bow-on	
			UNDERWAY so NAVIGATION; NOT under POWER so NO STEAMING. RED over GREEN is seldom seen; and not to be used with a mast lantern (no room for both!)
			Under TWENTY metres can have TRICOLOUR
			Under SEVEN metres can have SINGLE white
			Treated as power-driven vessel even if sails set. CONE = ARROW pointing down to propeller (under power)

over 12m   under 12m

			Memory aids and comments
sailing		anchored	
			Sides + stern when sailing Sides + stern + steaming when motoring Ranges (miles): Over 50 m: steaming = 6; others = 3 Ranges (miles): Over 20 m: steaming = 5; others = 2
			Bow lantern + stern OR mast lantern when sailing. Bow lantern + stern + steaming when motoring. Under TWENTY has TRICOLOUR (mast) or BICOLOUR (bow). Ranges (miles): Under 20 m: steaming = 3; others = 2
			Bow lantern + stern OR mast lantern when sailing. Bow lantern + WHITE when motoring. Under TWELVE has TWO in ONE (steam and stern) WHITE. Ranges (miles): Under 12 m: all lights = 2; except sidelights = 1

20 FISHING (Rule 26)

Vessel	Lights shown	Views
		side-on
VESSEL TRAWLING	☆ GREEN over WHITE (in place of steaming) ☆ aft steaming (optional if under 50 m) ☆ navigation (if making way) Shape = TWO CONES point-to-point OR: basket (if under 20 m)	 port side, over 50m
VESSEL FISHING (other than trawling)	☆ RED over WHITE ☆ navigation (if making way) ☆ WHITE towards gear (if gear more than 150 m long) Shape = as vessel trawling + CONE (point up) towards gear (if gear more than 150 m long)	 stopped, gear under 150m

VESSELS FISHING IN CLOSE PROXIMITY Optional Additional Signals

Vessel	Lights shown
TRAWLERS shooting nets	☆ WHITE over WHITE Shape = CODE FLAG Z:
TRAWLERS hauling nets	☆ WHITE over RED Shape = CODE FLAG G:
TRAWLERS when nets caught on bottom	☆ RED over RED (NUC) Shape = CODE FLAG P:
TRAWLERS pair trawling	☆ Searchlights forward towards each other Shape = CODE FLAG T:
PURSE SEINERS when hampered by gear	☆ TWO vertical isophase YELLOWS (flashing alternately)

bow-on	stern-on	stopped	**Memory aids**
			WHITE FISH under the GREEN sea. When STOPPED we can think of a TRAWLER as being MOORED by her NET, so NOT UNDERWAY. Hence NAVIGATION when MAKING WAY. Trawlers fish on the MOVE, hence GREEN over white for GO
			These vessels generally fish when stopped, hence RED over WHITE = STOPPED over WHITE fish. Same comments as trawlers regarding NAVIGATION when MAKING WAY. Shape = X marks the spot where fish are. CONE points up towards net on surface

Views			**Memory aids**
making way	stern	bow, over 50m	ALL CLEAR to go fishing
stopped	stern	bow, over 50m	Net often hauled on approaching navigation danger; hence PILOT lights shown
under 50m	over 50m		Vessel is clearly NOT UNDER COMMAND; hence NUC lights
			Searchlights give ARROW of light in direction of TRAVEL; keep outside the arrow as vessels joined by net. See International Code for details of flags
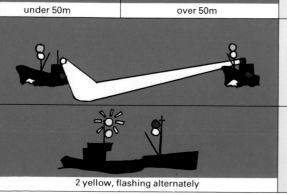 2 yellow, flashing alternately			TWO EQUAL GOLD coins in a PURSE; spend ONE AT A TIME

21 NOT UNDER COMMAND OR RESTRICTED MANOEUVRABILITY (Rule 27)

Vessel	Lights shown
NOT UNDER COMMAND	☆ NUC ☆ navigation (if making way) Shape = TWO vertical BALLS
RESTRICTED IN MANOEUVRABILITY	☆ Restricted ☆ power (if making way) ☆ anchor (if anchored) Shape = RESTRICTED + ANCHOR BALL (if anchored)
UNDERWATER OPERATIONS (e.g. dredging, surveying, diving)	☆ Restricted ☆ power (if making way) ☆ RED over RED on obstructed side ☆ GREEN over GREEN on clear side Shape = RESTRICTED + TWO vertical BALLS on obstructed side + TWO vertical DIAMONDS on clear side
MINE-CLEARANCE OPERATIONS	☆ THREE GREENS in TRIANGLE forward ☆ power (if underway) ☆ anchor (if anchored) Shape = THREE BALLS in TRIANGLE forward + ANCHOR BALL (if anchored)
DIVING OPERATIONS (when vessel cannot show lights and shapes for underwater operations)	☆ Restricted Shape = Rigid board of Code FLAG A (1 m high)

RESTRICTED VESSELS less than 12 m long are not required to show these lights or shapes (except diving vessels)

Views			Memory aids
making way	stopped	bow	TWO REDS = TOO DANGERous to COMMAND. All vessels keep clear of those not under command, so NAVIGATION is all that is needed to indicate making way. BALLS replace RED lights by day
making way, over 50m	stern	making way, under 50m	RED WHITE RED = Red When Restricted. BALLS replace RED lights; DIAMOND replaces WHITE light. POWER when MAKING WAY (i.e. STEAMING along). Restricted lights may be placed above aft steaming light
bow, stopped	making way, over 50m, starboard, foul side		As above. Vessel likely to be attached to seabed when stopped; hence no need for ANCHOR lights. TWO REDS = TOO DANGERous to approach; TWO GREENS = all CLEAR. BALLS are RED; DIAMONDS are CLEAR
underway, under 50m	stern	anchored	Shape matches function lights. Do not approach within 1000 m on any side; divers may be down: equipment may be streamed
night	day: shape		As restricted. These lights/shapes shown by *any size* diving boat

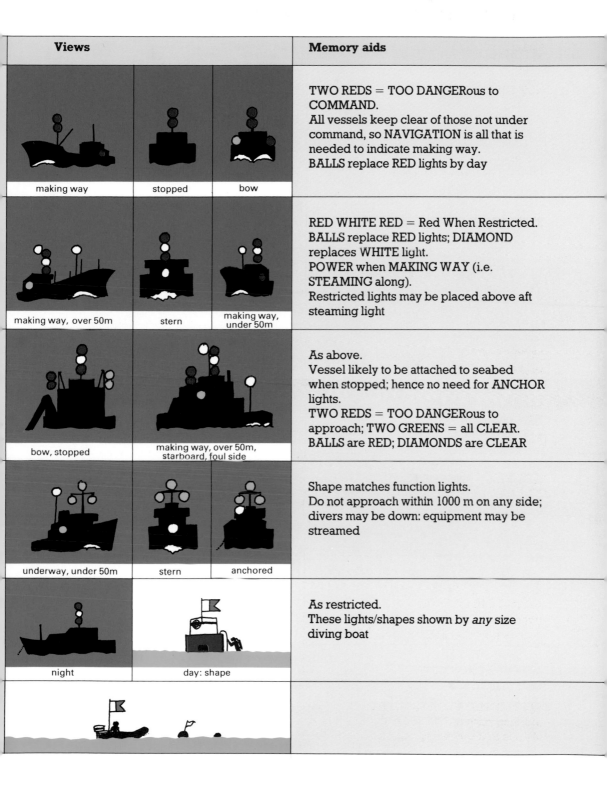

22 SUNDRY VESSELS (Rules 28–31)

Vessel	Lights shown
VESSEL CONSTRAINED BY DRAFT	☆ power ☆ THREE vertical REDS Shape = Vertical CYLINDER
PILOT VESSEL ON DUTY	☆ WHITE over RED ☆ navigation (if underway) ☆ anchor (if anchored) Shape = Code FLAG H (or rigid board) + ANCHOR BALL (if anchored)
VESSEL AT ANCHOR	☆ WHITE forward ☆ WHITE aft (lower than forward one) ☆ lights illuminating decks (optional if less than 100 m) Shape = ANCHOR BALL
VESSEL AT ANCHOR Less than 50 m	☆ as above (excluding deck lights) OR ☆ WHITE where best seen Shape = ANCHOR BALL
VESSEL AT ANCHOR Less than 7 m if clear of fairway	☆ lights and shape optional
VESSEL AGROUND	☆ anchor ☆ NUC Shape = THREE vertical BALLS
VESSEL AGROUND Less than 12 m	☆ lights and shapes optional
SEAPLANE	☆ power (if under way on water) ☆ anchor (if anchored) ☆ others according to circumstance OR as close as possible to these

Lights & Shapes (Part C)

Views	Memory aids
making way, over 50m / **stern** / **bow 1** / **bow 2**	POWER because UNDER POWER. TRIPLE DECKER DEEP = THREE REDS for DEEP draft. DEEP cylinder = DEEP draft. Function lights may be placed above aft steaming light
anchored / **stern** / **bow** / **shape**	PILOT wears a WHITE cap above RED face. WHITE over RED: the PILOT's ahead. Lights match flag colours
	WHITES indicate presence and extent of vessel. Bow is normally higher than stern, so forward light high. Decklights connect two distant anchor lights to show it is one ship, not two. ANCHOR BALL distinguishes from moving vessel in daytime
	Small vessel (less than 12 m) may have single anchor light at masthead utilising SINGLE WHITE shown when motoring
	Very small vessel anchored clear of other shipping is unlikely to be hazard, so no need for signals Under SEVEN when anchored CLEAR: NO need for LIGHTS to show you're here
	Attached to seabed, so ANCHOR light. NOT exactly UNDER COMMAND, so NUC. THREE BALLS = NUC BALLS + ANCHOR BALL
	A small vessel aground is unlikely to be a hazard hence no need for signals
	Treated as a power-driven vessel when afloat but lights may be placed unusually: STEAMING may be very low; SIDES wide apart (on wingtips)

23 IDENTIFYING LIGHTS AT SEA

It is important to realise, while looking at these neat diagrams of lights, that all too often in real life this is not what you will see. Apart from the possibility that one or more lights may be defunct (most unlikely in a large ship, but not unknown in small ones), there are two basic considerations that you must bear in mind.

The first problem is that not all vessels adhere properly to the prescribed arcs, intensities and positions of lights, so from certain angles their lights may create a quite confusing, or even false impression. All-around function lights tend to suffer from blind spots caused by masts and superstructure. Sometimes two lights are fitted, fore and aft of the mast, to provide all-around visibility, but often this merely increases confusion when seen from the side.

The second problem is that cabin lights and deck lights frequently obscure navigation lights at all but very close ranges. Passenger ferries and fishing boats are the worst culprits.

A certain amount of commonsense and experience must therefore be applied to the identification of lights. You should take into account such things as the time and place of encountering a vessel, its apparent speed and the depth of water; weighing up these factors (and others) will often help in the identification of doubtful combinations of lights. You should watch for a while to see if lights dodge back and forth behind masts, or disappear behind waves. Consider the relative distances apart of lights, to judge

→ On some vessels the all-around function lights are obscured by the mast, and two lights are fitted to prevent a blind spot. The effect can be confusing.

whether they are at the masthead, pulpit or wheelhouse, and whether they are grouped together intentionally or merely in accidental groupings. Take account of the varying ranges of different lights (see Chapter 15) to gauge which are most likely to be visible. Steaming lights, for example, are invariably visible long before sidelights come into view. Naval vessels, especially frigates and submarines, can be most confusing at times. A frigate will often display a single steaming light whatever her length, because she has only one mast. A submarine will seem much smaller than she is, partly because she is so low in the water and partly because her sidelights and aft steaming lights are usually well forward. A submarine may also have steaming lights forward that are lower than her sidelights, so take care.

Apparent vertical groups of lights must be treated with caution, because they are often hung relatively low down in rigging so that the sidelights, for example, may appear to be part of the group. The relationships between lights will also alter according to the aspect of the vessel. The lowest lights of apparently vertical groups should always be considered as possible navigation or anchor lights. Similarly, white upper lights of groups may be steaming lights.

In the next chapter a selection of ambiguous lights and groups of lights are listed together with both probable and possible meanings. Do not try to memorise these light groupings; they are intended simply to encourage the sort of lateral thinking that you will need if you are to assess all the possible meanings of any particular group of lights seen at sea.

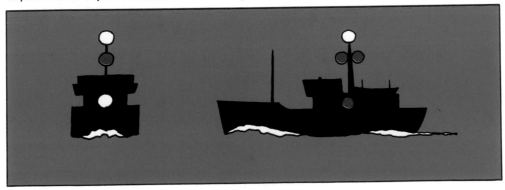

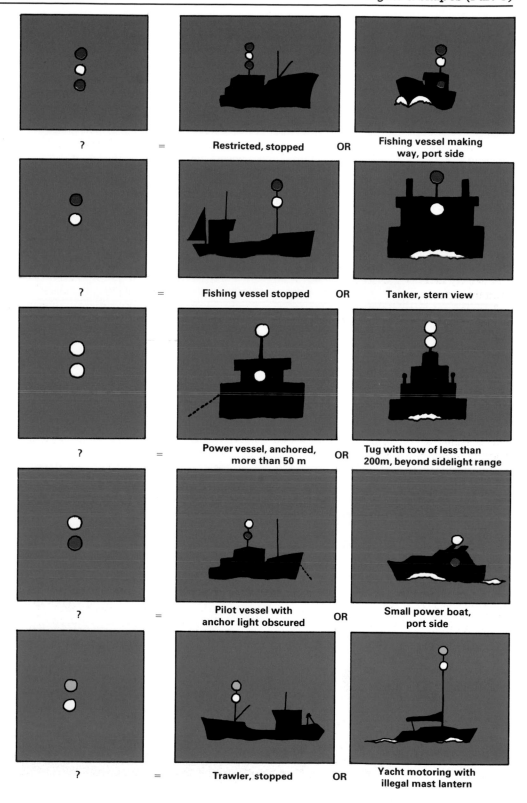

? = **Restricted, stopped** OR **Fishing vessel making way, port side**

? = **Fishing vessel stopped** OR **Tanker, stern view**

? = **Power vessel, anchored, more than 50 m** OR **Tug with tow of less than 200m, beyond sidelight range**

? = **Pilot vessel with anchor light obscured** OR **Small power boat, port side**

? = **Trawler, stopped** OR **Yacht motoring with illegal mast lantern**

24 CLARIFYING AMBIGUOUS LIGHTS

AMBIGUOUS LIGHTS

☆ ONE WHITE	○	? STERNLIGHT of all types of vessels, tows etc (1) ? ANCHOR LIGHT of any vessel anchored (2) ? very small boat under sail, power or oars (3) ? STEAMING LIGHT of small power vessel beyond sidelight range (4) ? dracone under tow (5)
☆ TWO WHITE (vertical)	○ ○	? large power vessel head-on with fore and aft STEAMING LIGHTS (6) ? STEAMING LIGHTS of a tug less than 50 m long with a tow of less than 200 m (7)
☆ TWO WHITE (horizontal)	○ ○	? STEAMING LIGHTS of power vessel side on, with aft light higher (8) ? ANCHOR LIGHTS of large vessel side on with aft light lower (9) ? semi-submerged tow side-on, with tug lights ahead (10)
☆ THREE WHITE (vertical)	○ ○ ○	? STEAMING LIGHTS of a tug less than 50 m long with a tow of more than 200 m (11) ? STEAMING LIGHTS of a tug more than 50 m long, head-on with a tow of less than 200 m (12)
☆ WHITE over RED	○ ●	? power vessel less than 50 m long, port side (13) ? pilot vessel at anchor, with anchor light obscured (14)
☆ ONE RED	●	? sailing or rowing vessel port side (15) ? fixed navigation light on shore (16)
☆ TWO RED (vertical)	● ●	? vessel not under command and stopped (17) ? vessel aground, with anchor light obscured (18) ? sailing vessel (port side) showing mast lantern and low sidelight (19) ? fixed navigation lights on end of jetty (20)
☆ RED over WHITE	● ○	? vessel fishing and stopped (21) ? yacht motoring illegally with mast lantern, port side (22) ? vessel carrying explosives, stern-on (23)
☆ TWO RED over WHITE	● ● ○	? vessel aground, head-on or stern-on (24) ? vessel not under command but making way, stern-on (25)
☆ RED WHITE RED	● ○ ●	? restricted vessel stopped (26) ? fishing vessel making way, port side (27)
☆ GREEN over WHITE	◐ ○	? trawler less than 50 m long, stopped (28) ? yacht motorsailing illegally with mast lantern, starboard side (29)

CLARIFYING THE LIGHTS

(1) will close more slowly than your speed
(2) will close at your speed; almost certainly with lots of deck and porthole lights
(3) is extremely unlikely to show any extraneous lights; watch for moving flashlight
(4) seek out sidelights through binoculars as you close
(5) look for tug lights to one side

(6) seek out both sidelights as you close; lights will move on change of aspect
(7) may show only one sidelight; lights will not move as aspect changes

(8) look for sidelights, and movement on change of aspect; vessel will have portlights but not decklights
(9) no sidelights; masses of decklights
(10) both same height; look for tug lights to one side

(11) the three whites will remain vertical with change of aspect
(12) the upper (aft) white light will part from other two with change of aspect

(13) lights probably a fair distance apart, but not always; check movement
(14) no movement; watch for anchor light as aspect changes

(15) vessel will move against the shore
(16) light will move very little against the shore; check chart

(17) keep well away
(18) check depth where lights are; watch for anchor light as aspect changes
(19) lights will be long way apart; SHOULD NOT OCCUR
(20) check chart and lack of movement

(21) will have masses of decklights in small space
(22) lights may be fair distance apart; no decklights; SHOULD NOT OCCUR
(23) closing speed should be low; red may move about with change of aspect

(24) check depth; probably many decklights
(25) reds may move with change of aspect; slow closing speed; unlikely deck lights

(26) lights should be equally spaced
(27) bottom red probably further apart than other two; may swing out of line

(28) lights close together; masses of decklights
(29) lights further apart, probably; no deck lights; SHOULD NOT OCCUR

25 SOUND SIGNALS AND DISTRESS SIGNALS

Rule 32: Definitions
Whistle = sound signal appliance complying with Annex III of the Collision Regulations
Short blast = 1 second
Long blast = 4-6 seconds

Rule 33: Equipment for sound signals
Vessel more than 100 m long: whistle; bell; gong (different sound from bell)
Vessel more than 12 m long: whistle; bell
Vessel less than 12 m long: some means of making sound signal (e.g. aerosol horn)

Rule 34: Manoeuvring and warning signals	
I am altering course to STARBOARD	1 short blast (·)
I am altering course to PORT	2 short blasts (· ·)
My engines are running ASTERN (but not necessarily making sternway)	3 short blasts (· · ·)
Are you taking enough avoiding action?	5 short blasts (· · · · ·)
(All the sound signals above may be supplemented by identical light signals, using flashes instead of blasts)	
I intend to OVERTAKE you (followed by)	2 long blasts (— —)
– on your starboard side	1 short blast (— — ·)
– on your PORT side	2 short blasts (— — · ·)
I agree to be OVERTAKEN	Morse code C (— · — ·)
I am approaching a bend in the channel	1 long blast (—)

All these sound signals should be used only when vessels are in sight of one another, allowing one second between blasts/flashes, and 10 seconds between signals. If you use a signalling light it should be an all-round WHITE with a visibility of five miles.

Rule 35: Sound signals in restricted visibility	
Power vessel underway	1 long blast every 2 minutes
Power vessel stopped	2 long blasts every 2 minutes
Sailing Fishing Constrained by draft Not under command Restricted Towing	1 long blast followed by 2 short blasts, every 2 minutes
Tow (if manned) (after tug signal)	Morse B (— · · ·) every 2 minutes

Sound signals in restricted visibility (continued)	
Anchored	5 secs ringing of bell forward every 1 minute (then 5 secs gong aft, if more than 100 metres long). May sound Morse R (· — ·) to warn approaching vessel
Aground	3 rings bell; then anchor signal; then 3 rings bell
Pilot vessels	suitable signal from above list; may also sound Morse H (· · · ·)
Vessel restricted or fishing when at anchor	Morse D (— · ·) every 2 minutes

[Vessels less than 12m long are not obliged to give the above signals, but they must make *some* sound every 2 minutes]

Annex IV: Distress Signals

1 Gun or explosive signal fired about once a minute
2 Continuous sounding of foghorn
3 Rockets/shells firing single red stars at short intervals
4 Morse S O S (· · · — — — · · ·) by any means (light/sound etc)
5 The word MAYDAY on a radio-telephone
6 International code flags N above C
7 A square flag and a round shape hoisted together
8 Flames on the vessel (such as an oil-soaked rag on boathook)
9 Red flares – rocket, parachute or hand
10 Orange smoke signal
11 Slow, repeated raising and lowering of outstretched arms
12 Built-in alarm signals from radio transmitters
13 Signals from Emergency Position Indicating Radio Beacons (EPIRBS)
14 Approved signals from radio transmitters

Signals for identification from the air

1 Orange canvas marked with black square and circle
2 Dye marker

Rule 36: Signals to attract attention

You can make light or sound signals to attract the attention of another vessel, or shine searchlights in the direction of danger. The signals must not be capable of being mistaken for any in these rules, or for any navigation light. For this reason, high-intensity strobe-type lights should not be used. Lights must *not* be shone at the bridge of a ship, because of the risk of ruining the night vision of the man on watch.

This rule permits you to shine a flashlight on your sails or towards an approaching vessel to warn her of your presence. If necessary, you can also use white flares.

Rule 37: Distress signals

Vessels in distress and requiring assistance shall use the signals in Annex IV, as listed on the left. They should be used only when there is grave danger to the vessel or crew. For less urgent problems, see the International Code (page 58).

QUESTIONS: RISK OF COLLISION UNDER SAIL

Where correct lights may not be available they are prefixed (C); alternative lights are prefixed (A). The lights described are the minimum required; often those for larger vessels may be used.

QUESTIONS			ANSWERS
YOUR VESSEL	VIEW	LIGHTS SEEN	YOUR LIGHTS
10 m; port tack; closehauled; in narrow channel	wind		Mast lantern Ch. 19
23 m; port tack; broad reaching; across traffic lane			Navigation RED over GREEN Ch. 19
8 m; starboard tack; hove-to; jib and mainsail			Mast lantern Ch. 19
6·5 m; port tack; running; jib and mainsail			WHITE; to avert collision Ch. 19
3·5 m; dinghy; under oars; no mast			WHITE; to avert collision Ch. 19
9·5 m; port tack; towing another; beam reaching			Mast lantern Searchlight on tow Ch. 18, 19
13 m; starboard tack; running; under spinnaker			Mast lantern Ch. 19
8 m; dismasted; stopped; no engine			(C) NUC Navigation Ch. 19, 21
7·5 m; starboard tack; jib and mainsail; engine in gear			WHITE Bow lantern Day = CONE point down Ch. 17
12 m; broken rudder; making way port tack; mainsail; jib backed			(C) NUC + navigation Mast lantern Ch. 19, 21

Where technically correct action may differ from realistic but seamanlike action both are given, prefixed (C) and (S) accordingly. For more details see Introduction and Chapter 12.

VESSEL SEEN	CORRECT ACTION
Sailing boat; running; uncertain which tack *Ch. 19*	Assume she is on starboard tack; so keep clear; tack onto starboard and stand clear of her; then tack back to port and go astern of her *Ch. 8*
Power-vessel longer than 50 m; starboard bow *Ch. 17*	She follows traffic lane, so do not hinder; come hard on the wind and cross astern of her; if this is insufficient, tack and stand clear *Ch.6*
Trawler longer than 50 m; head-on; making way; towing net *Ch. 20*	She has right of way; let draw jib and sail clear of her path *Ch. 12*
Tug shorter than 50 m with tow less than 200 m; port side; lights of tow not visible *Ch. 18*	(C) You have right of way; hold your course. (S) Look for lights of tow astern of tug; gybe onto starboard early; go astern of tow *Ch. 12, 18*
Pilot vessel; port side *Ch. 22*	(C) You have right of way; hold your course. (S) show light; turn 180°; row furiously; pilot vessels are often high speed launches *Ch. 12*
Sailing vessel shorter than 20 m; head-on; on starboard tack *Ch. 19*	She has right of way; keep clear. Bear hard away so tow will clear her stern; illuminate towline and tow *Ch. 8, 18*
Tug shorter than 50 m with tow longer than 200 m; unable to alter course; port side *Ch. 18*	Keep clear; hand spinnaker if necessary. Look far astern of tug for lights of tow; harden up round to stbd; pass astern of tow *Ch. 12, 18*
Power-vessel longer than 50 m; head-on; carrying explosives *Ch. 17*	(C) You have right of way if showing NUC lights. (S) If no NUC lights fire white flare to warn, then flash U, F, M or D accordingly *Ch. 12, 25, 29*
Hovercraft or submarine; starboard side *Ch. 17, 24*	You are classed as power-driven vessel. You have right of way; hold course. Hovercraft very fast; show attention signal *Ch. 1, 11, 25*
Dredger etc; diamonds show clear side *Ch. 21*	(C) If Showing NUC lights you have right of way. (S) She probably cannot get out of your way; you probably won't weather her clear side; tack onto starboard and make up to weather *Ch. 12*

QUESTIONS: RISK OF COLLISION UNDER POWER

Where correct lights may not be available they are prefixed (C); alternative lights are prefixed (A). The lights described are the minimum required; often those for larger vessels may be used.

QUESTIONS			ANSWERS
YOUR VESSEL	**VIEW**	**LIGHTS SEEN**	**YOUR LIGHTS**
9 m; planing; motor cruiser; making 24 knots			WHITE Bow lantern Ch. 17
5 m; open dinghy; outboard engine making 6 knots			WHITE Ch. 17
18 m; aux yacht; under power only; making 8 knots			Steaming + stern Bow lantern Ch. 17
10 m; fishing boat loaded with nets; steaming home at 8 knots			WHITE Bow lantern (No fishing lights) Ch. 19
6·5 m; motor launch; angling; stopped in water			WHITE (NO fishing lights) Ch. 1, 17
12 m; motor cruiser; broken steering; making 3 knots			(C) NUC + navigation Steaming + stern Bow lantern Ch. 17, 21
6 m; rubber dinghy; working divers; outboard stopped			Restricted Day = rigid CODE FLAG A Ch. 21
11·5 m; inshore trawler; towing net; making 2 knots			GREEN over WHITE Navigation Day = BASKET Ch. 20
22 m; motor cruiser; on passage; making 12 knots			Steaming Navigation Ch. 17
11 m; motor cruiser; towing 6·5 m yacht; making 5 knots			WHITE Bow lantern Searchlight on tow Ch. 17, 18

Where technically correct action may differ from realistic but seamanlike action both are given, prefixed (C) and (S) accordingly. For more details see Introduction and Chapter 12.

VESSEL SEEN	CORRECT ACTION
Power-vessel shorter than 50 m; port side Ch. 17	You must keep clear; alter to starboard; pass clear astern Ch. 11
Fishing vessel (not trawler); making way; port side Ch. 20	You must keep clear; alter to starboard; pass under his stern; watch for any sudden change of course Ch. 4, 12
Power-vessel longer than 50 m; constrained by draft; starboard side Ch. 17, 22	(C) Your right of way; she on your port side. (C) You should not impede her safe passage. (S) Alter hard to port early; pass astern Ch. 4, 11, 12
Trawler longer than 50 m; starboard side; making way Ch. 20	You are not 'engaged in fishing'; but she is. You are normal power-vessel; keep clear. Alter to port; pass astern Ch. 1, 4, 12
Sailing vessel; starboard side; probably a large one Ch. 19	You are not 'engaged in fishing'; you are normal power-vessel; keep clear; motor away at right angles to her course Ch. 1, 4, 12
Restricted vessel; making way; starboard side Ch. 21	(C) If NUC lights shown you have right of way. (S) She may be more restricted than you. (S) Alter to port early; pass well astern Ch. 4, 12
Not under command; making way; port side Ch. 21	You must keep clear. Get divers aboard immediately; turn 180°; motor fast at right angles to his course Ch. 4, 12
Mine-clearance vessel longer than 50 m; underway; port side Ch. 21	You must keep clear. Alter hard to starboard; pass at least 1000 m clear and astern Ch. 12, 21
Tug with tow alongside; stern view Ch. 18	You must keep clear. Alter to starboard if way is clear; or to port. Pass well clear down his side Ch. 9
Power-vessel longer than 50 m; almost head-on; beyond sidelight range (3 m) Ch. 15, 17	Both alter hard to starboard; pass down port sides. Doubtful crossing situation? Take same action. Illuminate towline and tow Ch. 4, 10, 18

QUESTIONS: GENERAL RULE OF THE ROAD

1 What is the maximum length of sailing boat that can use a mast (tricolour) lantern?

2 If risk of collision exists, what should be the action of the stand-on vessel?

3 What sound signal should be given by a vessel agreeing to be overtaken?

4 What is meant by the term 'underway'?

5 What precisely is implied by the phrase 'in sight of one another'?

6 How would you determine whether a risk of collision exists?

7 What should be the usual action of a power vessel required to give way?

8 In what manner should small vessels cross traffic lanes?

9 Risk of collision exists with a ship ahead on radar alone. What should you not do?

10 What is meant by, and *not* meant by, a sound signal of three short blasts?

11 What does Rule 2 in principle state?

12 What is the only distress signal that requires no material or equipment?

13 How is the windward side of a sailing vessel defined?

14 What must a vessel shining a light towards another vessel avoid doing?

15 What must a sailing vessel not do to a vessel following a traffic lane?

16 How do the rules apply if she cannot, for some reason, comply with this?

17 Describe the lights and shapes referred to in this book as 'restricted'.

18 What is the approved rescue signal for identification from the air?

19 What sound signal is given by a vessel over 100 metres long at anchor in fog?

20 What signals may be shown by a purse seiner hampered by her gear?

21 What signal shall specifically *not* be used to attract attention? Why?

22 Give the minimum ranges of lights for a vessel over 50 m long and between 12m and 20 m.

23 What must a power-driven vessel do with her engines in restricted visibility?

24 What is a towing light, and where precisely is it situated?

25 Where is the cut-off line for the arcs of masthead and navigation lights?

26 What does a sound signal of one short blast signify?

27 What are NUC lights? Describe them, and their daytime equivalent.

28 What lights and shapes are to be shown by a 10 m yacht that is aground?

29 What type and range of light may be used to flash manoeuvring signals?

30 What should a sailing vessel do with her rig in restricted visibility?

31 What may a stand-on vessel do if the other does not seem to be taking action?

32 What should she not do, if possible, in a power vessel crossing situation?

33 In doubt as to whether you are in another's overtaking arc, what do you assume?

34 What vessels make the following sound signal in fog: (— · ·) every 2 minutes?

35 On which side of a narrow channel should vessels proceed?

36 What arc is covered by the GREEN GIVE-WAY SECTOR?

37 Should a yacht motoring use a tricolour mast lantern above a steaming light? Why?

38 Name three types of vessel that could be restricted in their manoeuvrability.

39 What is the recognised distress signal in Morse Code?

40 Give a sound signal made by a vessel wanting to overtake on your port side.

41 Give the maximum ranges of lights for a vessel between 20 m and 50 m long, and less than 12 m.

42 To what vessels do the Collision Regulations apply?

43 What lights should be installed on a 32ft yacht to cover sailing and motoring?

44 How long is a prolonged blast?

45 What vessels must a sailing boat keep clear of?

46 Which restricted vessel less than 12 m long is *not* exempted from displaying restricted lights?

47 What lights should be shown by a 43ft yacht that is aground?

48 Under what circumstances must a yacht not display RED over GREEN at the masthead?

49 What is the closest that a mineclearance vessel should be approached?

50 What identity signal may a pilot vessel on duty make by sound in fog?

ANSWERS

1 20 metres (Twenty for Tricolour) *Ch. 9*

2 Hold course and speed (so give-way vessel can judge her progress) *Ch.12*

3 — · — · (Morse code C: see International Code meaning in Appendix) *Ch. 25*

4 Not attached to the ground or seabed (not necessarily moving, however) *Ch.1*

5 Observable by eye (i.e. *not* on radar alone) *Ch. 1*

6 If compass bearing of other vessel remains steady, risk of collision exists *Ch.3*

7 Alter course to starboard; pass astern of other vessel if at all possible *Ch. 4*

8 On a *heading* at right angles to the flow of traffic (not the ground track) *Ch. 6*

9 Do not alter to port; if you do, you risk crossing ahead, or the other vessel turning to starboard *Ch.13*

10 My engines are going astern; but my vessel is *not* necessarily doing the same *Ch. 25*

11 The rules shall not override principles of safety and sound seamanship *Ch. 1*

12 Repeated raising and lowering of the arms (a very useful signal) *Ch. 25*

13 Opposite that on which the mainsail (or largest fore-and-aft sail) is carried *Ch.8*

14 Shining it onto the wheelhouse and into the eyes of Officer on watch *Ch. 25*

15 Impede her progress *Ch.6*

16 Normal rules in Section 2 apply (as though traffic lane did not exist) *Ch. 6*

17 RED over WHITE over RED lights; BALL over DIAMOND over BALL (black shapes) *Ch. 16*

18 Orange canvas showing black square and circle *Ch. 25*

19 5-sec ringing bell forward, then 5-sec sounding of gong aft; every 1 minute *Ch.25*

20 2 vertical isophase yellows, flashing alternately *Ch. 20*

21 Quick-flashing strobe light; too similar to North Cardinal buoy *Ch. 25*

22 Longer than 50 m: masthead 6, others 3. 12-20 m: masthead 3, others 2 (miles) *Ch. 15*

23 Have them ready for immediate manoeuvring *Ch. 13*

24 Yellow showing over same arc as sternlight; above sternlight *Ch. 15*

25 22½° abaft each beam *Ch. 7*

26 I am altering course to starboard *Ch. 25*

27 Two vertical reds (all-round); two vertical black balls *Ch. 16*

28 None; vessels less than 12 m long are exempt from aground signals *Ch. 22*

29 All-round white; 5 miles *Ch. 25*

30 Have it ready for immediate manoeuvring; i.e. no spinnakers, preventers etc. *Ch. 13*

31 Take action herself to avoid collision *Ch. 12*

32 Alter to port for a vessel on her port side (as it may turn to starboard into her) *Ch. 12*

33 You assume that you are in it, and keep clear accordingly *Ch. 9*

34 Sailing; fishing; towing; not under command; restricted; constrained *Ch. 25*

35 Starboard side *Ch.5*

36 Ahead round starboard side to 22½° abaft the beam *Ch. 7*

37 NO; port side looks like a fishing boat, starboard side a trawler *Ch. 20*

38 Flying aircraft; replenishing; dredging; unwieldy tow; cable-laying etc. *Ch. 12*

39 · · · — — — · · · (S O S) *Ch. 25*

40 — — · · (2 long blasts = request to overtake; 2 shorts = on port side) *Ch. 25*

41 20-50 m: masthead 5, others 2. Shorter than 12 m: masthead 2, stern 2, sides 1 *Ch. 15*

42 All vessels on the high seas and waters connected with them *Ch. 1*

43 Mast lantern; all-round white; bow lantern; stern *Ch. 19*

44 Between 4 and 6 seconds *Ch. 25*

45 Not under command; restricted; constrained; fishing *Ch. 12*

46 Vessel working divers (to preserve safety of divers in water) *Ch. 21*

47 Anchor light; NUC lights (2 vertical reds) *Ch. 22*

48 When using a mast lantern (all lights will be too close together) *Ch.19*

49 1000 metres (may be working divers or outlying gear) *Ch. 21*

50 Morse H (· · · ·) (see page 58 for International Code meaning) *Ch. 25*

COMMUNICATIONS

Code flag	Phonetic alphabet	Morse	International Code
	A ALPHA	· —	I have a diver down – keep clear
	B BRAVO	— · · ·	I am loading, unloading or carrying dangerous cargo
	C CHARLIE	— · — ·	Yes; affirmative
	D DELTA	— · ·	Keep clear of me, I am manoeuvring with difficulty
	E ECHO	·	I am altering course to starboard
	F FOXTROT	· · — ·	I am disabled – communicate with me
	G GOLF	— — ·	I require a pilot – OR – I am hauling nets (trawlers in company)
	H HOTEL	· · · ·	I have a pilot on board
	I INDIA	· ·	I am altering course to port
	J JULIET	· — — —	I am on fire with dangerous cargo – keep clear
	K KILO	— · —	I wish to communicate with you
	L LIMA	· — · ·	You should stop your vessel instantly
	M MIKE	— —	My vessel is stopped and making no way
	N NOVEMBER	— ·	No; negative
	O OSCAR	— — —	Man overboard
	P PAPA	· — — ·	Vessel is about to sail – OR – my nets are caught on the bottom
	Q QUEBEC	— — · —	My vessel is healthy and I require free pratique
	R ROMEO	· — ·	No meaning except by sound in fog (see Ch. 25)
	S SIERRA	· · ·	My engines are going astern
	T TANGO	—	Keep clear, I am engaged in pair trawling
	U UNIFORM	· · —	You are standing into danger
	V VICTOR	· · · —	I require assistance
	W WHISKY	· — —	I require medical assistance
	X X-RAY	— · · —	Stop what you are doing and watch for my signals
	Y YANKEE	— · — —	I am dragging my anchor
	Z ZULU	— — · ·	I require a tug – OR – I am shooting nets

THE COLLISION REGULATIONS

PART A. GENERAL

RULE 1

Application
(a) These Rules shall apply to all vessels upon the high seas and in all waters connected therewith navigable by seagoing vessels.
(b) Nothing in these Rules shall interfere with the operation of special rules made by an appropriate authority for roadsteads, harbours, rivers, lakes or inland waterways connected with the high seas and navigable by seagoing vessels. Such special rules shall conform as closely as possible to these Rules.
(c) Nothing in these Rules shall interfere with the operation of any special rules made by the Government of any State with respect to additional station or signal lights, shapes or whistle signals for ships of war and vessels proceeding under convoy, or with respect to additional station or signal lights or shapes for fishing vessels engaged in fishing as a fleet. These additional station or signal lights, shapes or whistle signals shall, so far as possible, be such that they cannot be mistaken for any light, shape or signal authorised elsewhere under these Rules.
(d) Traffic separation schemes may be adopted by the Organisation for the purpose of these Rules.
(e) Whenever the Government concerned shall have determined that a vessel of special construction or purpose cannot comply fully with the provisions of any of these Rules with respect to the number, position, range or arc of visibility of lights or shapes, as well as to the disposition and characteristics of sound-signalling appliances, such vessel shall comply with such other provisions in regard to the number, position, range of arc of visibility of lights or shapes, as well as to the disposition and characteristics of sound-signalling appliances, as her Government shall have determined to be the closest possible compliance with these Rules in respect of that vessel.

RULE 2

Responsibility
(a) Nothing in these Rules shall exonerate any vessel, or the owner, master or crew thereof, from the consequences of any neglect to comply with these Rules or of the neglect of any precaution which may be required by the ordinary practice of seamen, or by the special circumstances of the case.
(b) In construing and complying with these Rules due regard shall be had to all dangers of navigation and collision and to any special circumstances, including the limitations of the vessels involved, which may make a departure from these Rules necessary to avoid immediate danger.

RULE 3

General definitions
For the purpose of these Rules, except where the context otherwise requires:
(a) The word "vessel" includes every description of water craft, including non-displacement craft and seaplanes, used or capable of being used as a means of transportation on water.
(b) The term "power-driven vessel" means any vessel propelled by machinery.
(c) The term "sailing vessel" means any vessel under sail provided that propelling machinery, if fitted, is not being used.
(d) The term "vessel engaged in fishing" means any vessel fishing with nets, lines, trawls or other fishing apparatus which restrict manoeuvrability, but does not include a vessel fishing with trolling lines or other fishing apparatus which do not restrict manoeuvrability.
(e) The word "seaplane" includes any aircraft designed to manoeuvre on the water.
(f) The term "vessel not under command" means a vessel which through some exceptional circumstances is unable to manoeuvre as required by these Rules and is therefore unable to keep out of the way of another vessel.
(g) The term "vessel restricted in her ability to manoeuvre" means a vessel which from the nature of her work is restricted in her ability to manoeuvre as required by these Rules and is therefore unable to keep out of the way of another vessel.
   The term "vessels restricted in their ability to manoeuvre" shall include but not be limited to:
   (i) a vessel engaged in laying, servicing or picking up a navigation mark, submarine cable or pipeline;
   (ii) a vessel engaged in dredging, surveying or underwater operations;
   (iii) a vessel engaged in replenishment or transferring persons, provisions or cargo while underway;
   (iv) a vessel engaged in the launching or recovery of aircraft;
   (v) a vessel engaged in mine-clearance operations;
   (vi) a vessel engaged in a towing operation such as severely restricts the towing vessel and her tow in their ability to deviate from their course.
(h) The term "vessel constrained by her draught" means a power-driven vessel which, because of her draught in relation to the available depth and width of navigable water, is severely restricted in her ability to deviate from the course she is following.
(i) The word "underway" means that a vessel is not at anchor, or made fast to the shore, or aground.
(j) The words "length" and "breadth" of a vessel mean her length overall and greatest breadth.
(k) Vessels shall be deemed to be in sight of one another only when one can be observed visually from the other.
(l) The term "restricted visibility" means any condition in which visibility is restricted by fog, mist, falling snow, heavy rainstorms, sandstorms or any other similar causes.

PART B. STEERING AND SAILING RULES

Section 1: Conduct of vessels in any condition of visibility

RULE 4

Application
Rules in this Section apply in any condition of visibility.

RULE 5

Look-out
Every vessel shall at all times maintain a proper look-out by sight and hearing as well as by all available means appropriate in the prevailing circumstances and conditions so as to make a full appraisal of the situation and of the risk of collision.

RULE 6

Safe speed
Every vessel shall at all times proceed at a safe speed so that she can take proper and effective action to avoid collision and be stopped within a distance appropriate to the prevailing circumstance and conditions.
   In determining a safe speed the following factors shall be among those taken into account:
(a) By all vessels:
   (i) the state of visibility;
   (ii) the traffic density including concentrations of fishing vessels or any other vessels;
   (iii) the manoeuvrability of the vessel with special reference to stopping distance and turning ability in the prevailing conditions;
   (iv) at night the presence of background light such as from shore lights or from back scatter of her own lights;
   (v) the state of wind, sea and current, and the proximity of navigational hazards;
   (vi) the draught in relation to the available depth of water.
(b) Additionally, by vessels with operational radar:
   (i) the characteristics, efficiency and limitations of the radar equipment;
   (ii) any constraints imposed by the radar range scale in use;
   (iii) the effect on radar detection of the sea state, weather and other sources of interference;
   (iv) the possibility that small vessels, ice and other floating objects may not be detected by radar at an adequate range;
   (v) the number, location and movement of vessels detected by radar;
   (vi) the more exact assessment of the visibility that may be possible when radar is used to determine the range of vessels or other objects in the vicinity.

RULE 7

Risk of collision
(a) Every vessel shall use all available means appropriate to the prevailing circumstances and conditions to determine if risk of collision exists. If there is any doubt such risk shall be deemed to exist.
(b) Proper use shall be made of radar equipment if fitted and operational, including long-range scanning to obtain early warning of risk of collision and radar plotting or equivalent systematic observation of detected objects.
(c) Assumptions shall not be made on the basis of scanty information, especially scanty radar information.
(d) In determining if risk of collision exists the following considerations shall be among those taken into account:
   (i) such risk shall be deemed to exist if the compass bearing of an approaching vessel does not appreciably change;
   (ii) such risk may sometimes exist even when an appreciable bearing change is evident, particularly when approaching a very large vessel or a tow or when approaching a vessel at close range.

RULE 8

Action to avoid collision
(a) Any action taken to avoid collision shall, if the circumstances of the case admit, be positive, made in ample time and with due regard to the observance of good seamanship.
(b) Any alteration of course and/or speed to avoid collision shall, if the circumstances of the case

admit, be large enough to be readily apparent to another vessel observing visually or by radar; a succession of small alterations of course and/or speed should be avoided.

(c) If there is sufficient sea room, alteration of course alone may be the most effective action to avoid a close-quarters situation provided that it is made in good time, is substantial and does not result in another close-quarters situation.

(d) Action taken to avoid collision with another vessel shall be such as to result in passing at a safe distance. The effectiveness of the action shall be carefully checked until the other vessel is finally past and clear.

(e) If necessary to avoid collision or allow more time to assess the situation, a vessel shall slacken her speed or take all way off by stopping or reversing her means of propulsion.

(f) (i) A vessel which, by another of these rules, is required not to impeded the passage or safe passage of another vessel shall, when required by the circumstances of the case, take early action to allow sufficient sea room for the safe passage of the other vessel;

(ii) A vessel required not to impede the passage or safe passage of another vessel is not relieved of this obligation if approaching the other vessel so as to involve risk of collision and shall, when taking action, have full regard to the action which may be required by the rules of this part.

(iii) A vessel the passage of which is not to be impeded remains fully obliged to comply with the rules of this part when the two vessels are approaching one another so as to involve risk of collision.

RULE 9

Narrow channels

(a) A vessel proceeding along the course of a narrow channel or fairway shall keep as near to the outer limit of the channel or fairway which lies on her starboard side as is safe and practicable.

(b) A vessel of less than 20 metres in length or a sailing vessel shall not impede the passage of a vessel which can safely navigate only within a narrow channel or fairway.

(c) A vessel engaged in fishing shall not impede the passage of any other vessel navigating within a narrow channel or fairway.

(d) A vessel shall not cross a narrow channel or fairway if such crossing impedes the passage of a vessel which can safely navigate only within such channel or fairway. The latter vessel may use the sound signal prescribed in Rule 34 (d) if in doubt as to the intention of the crossing vessel.

(e) (i) In a narrow channel or fairway when overtaking can take place only if the vessel to be overtaken has to take action to permit safe passing, the vessel intending to overtake shall indicate her intention by sounding the appropriate signal prescribed in Rule 34 (c) (i). The vessel to be overtaken shall, if in agreement, sound the appropriate signal prescribed in Rule 34 (c) (ii) and take steps to permit safe passing. If in doubt she may sound the signals prescribed in Rule 34 (d).

(ii) This Rule does not relieve the overtaking vessel of her obligation under Rule 13.

(f) A vessel nearing a bend or an area of a narrow channel or fairway where other vessels may be obscured by an intervening obstruction shall navigate with particular alertness and caution and shall sound the appropriate signal prescribed in Rule 34 (e).

(g) Any vessel shall, if the circumstances of the case admit, avoid anchoring in a narrow channel.

RULE 10

Traffic separation schemes

(a) This Rule applies to traffic separation schemes adopted by the Organisation and does not relieve any vessel of her obligation under any other rule.

(b) A vessel using a traffic separation scheme shall:

(i) proceed in the appropriate traffic lane in the general direction of traffic flow for that lane;

(ii) so far as practicable keep clear of a traffic separation line or separation zone;

(iii) normally join or leave a traffic lane at the termination of the lane, but when joining or leaving from either side shall do so at as small an angle to the general direction of traffic flow as practicable.

(c) A vessel shall, so far as practicable, avoid crossing traffic lanes, but if obliged to do so shall cross on a heading as nearly as practicable at right angles to the general direction of traffic flow.

(d) Inshore traffic zones shall not normally be used by through traffic which can safely use the appropriate traffic lane within the adjacent traffic separation scheme.

However, vessels of less than 20 metres in length and sailing vessels may under all circumstances use inshore traffic zones.

(e) A vessel other than a crossing vessel or a vessel joining or leaving a lane shall not normally enter a separation zone or cross a separation line except:

(i) in case of emergency to avoid immediate danger;

(ii) to engage in fishing within a separation zone.

(f) A vessel navigating in areas near the terminations of traffic separation schemes shall do so with particular caution.

(g) A vessel shall so far as practicable avoid anchoring in a traffic separation scheme or in areas near its terminations.

(h) A vessel not using a traffic separation scheme shall avoid it by as wide a margin as is practicable.

(i) A vessel engaged in fishing shall not impede the passage of any vessel following a traffic lane.

(j) A vessel of less than 20 metres in length or a sailing vessel shall not impede the safe passage of a power-driven vessel following a traffic lane.

(k) A vessel restricted in her ability to manoeuvre when engaged in an operation for the maintenance of safety of navigation in a traffic separation scheme is exempted from complying with this Rule to the extent necessary to carry out the operation.

(l) A vessel restricted in her ability to manoeuvre when engaged in an operation for the laying, servicing or picking up of a submarine cable, within a traffic separation scheme, is exempted from complying with this Rule to the extent necessary to carry out the operation.

Section 2: Conduct of vessels in sight of one another

RULE 11

Application

Rules in this Section apply to vessels in sight of one another.

RULE 12

Sailing vessels

(a) When two sailing vessels are approaching one another, so as to involve risk of collision, one of them shall keep out of the way of the other as follows:

(i) when each has the wind on a different side,

the vessel which has the wind on the port side shall keep out of the way of the other;

(ii) when both have the wind on the same side, the vessel which is to windward shall keep out of the way of the vessel which is to leeward;

(iii) if a vessel with the wind on the port side sees a vessel to windward and cannot determine with certainty whether the other vessel has the wind on the port or on the starboard side, she shall keep out of the way of the other.

(b) For the purposes of this Rule the windward side shall be deemed to be the side opposite to that on which the mainsail is carried or, in the case of a square-rigged vessel, the side opposite to that on which the largest fore-and-aft sail is carried.

RULE 13

Overtaking

(a) Notwithstanding anything contained in the Rules of Part B, Sections I and II, any vessel overtaking any other shall keep out of the way of the vessel being overtaken.

(b) A vessel shall be deemed to be overtaking when coming up with another vessel from a direction more than 22.5 degrees abaft her beam, that is, in such a position with reference to the vessel she is overtaking, that at night she would be able to see only the sternlight of that vessel but neither of her sidelights.

(c) When a vessel is in any doubt as to whether she is overtaking another, she shall assume that this is the case and act accordingly.

(d) Any subsequent alteration of the bearing between the two vessels shall not make the overtaking vessel a crossing vessel within the meaning of these Rules or relieve her of the duty of keeping clear of the overtaken vessel until she is finally past and clear.

RULE 14

Head-on situation

(a) When two power-driven vessels are meeting on reciprocal or nearly reciprocal courses so as to involve risk of collision each shall alter her course to starboard so that each shall pass on the port side of the other.

(b) Such a situation shall be deemed to exist when a vessel sees the other ahead or nearly ahead and by night she could see the masthead lights of the other in a line or nearly in a line and/or both sidelights and by day she observes the corresponding aspect of the other vessel.

(c) When a vessel is in any doubt as to whether such a situation exists she shall assume that it does exist and act accordingly.

RULE 15

Crossing situation

When two power-driven vessels are crossing so as to involve risk of collision, the vessel which has the other on her own starboard side shall keep out of the way and shall, if the circumstances of the case admit, avoid crossing ahead of the other vessel.

RULE 16

Action by give-way vessel

Every vessel which is directed to keep out of the way of another vessel shall, so far as possible, take early and substantial action to keep well clear.

RULE 17

Action by stand-on vessel
(a) (i) Where one of two vessels is to keep out of the way the other shall keep her course and speed.
(ii) The latter vessel may however take action to avoid collision by her manoeuvre alone, as soon as it becomes apparent to her that the vessel required to keep out of the way is not taking appropriate action in compliance with these Rules.
(b) When, from any cause, the vessel required to keep her course and speed finds herself so close that collision cannot be avoided by the action of the give-way vessel alone, she shall take such action as will best aid to avoid collision.
(c) A power-driven vessel which takes action in a crossing situation in accordance with sub-paragraph (a) (ii) of this Rule to avoid collision with another power-driven vessel shall, if the circumstances of the case admit, not alter course to port for a vessel on her own port side.
(d) This Rule does not relieve the give-way vessel of her obligation to keep out of the way.

RULE 18

Responsibilities between vessels
Except where Rules 9, 10 and 13 otherwise require:
(a) A power-driven vessel underway shall keep out of the way of:
(i) a vessel not under command;
(ii) a vessel restricted in her ability to manoeuvre;
(iii) a vessel engaged in fishing.
(iv) a sailing vessel;
(b) A sailing vessel underway shall keep out of the way of:
(i) a vessel not under command;
(ii) a vessel restricted in her ability to manoeuvre;
(iii) a vessel engaged in fishing.
(c) A vessel engaged in fishing when underway shall as far as possible, keep out of the way of:
(i) A vessel not under command;
(ii) a vessel restricted in her ability to manoeuvre.
(d) (i) Any vessel other than a vessel not under command or a vessel restricted in her ability to manoeuvre shall, if the circumstances of the case admit, avoid impeding the safe passage of a vessel constrained by her draught, exhibiting the signals in Rule 28.
(ii) A vessel constrained by her draft shall navigate with particular caution having full regard to her special condition.
(e) A seaplane on the water shall, in general, keep well clear of all vessels and avoid impeding their navigation. In circumstances, however, where risk of collision exists, she shall comply with the Rules of this Part.

Section 3: Conduct of vessels in restricted visibility

RULE 19

Conduct of vessels in restricted visibility
(a) This Rule applies to vessels not in sight of one another when navigating in or near an area of restricted visibility.
(b) Every vessel shall proceed at a safe speed adapted to the prevailing circumstances and conditions of restricted visibility. A power-driven vessel shall have her engines ready for immediate manoeuvre.
(c) Every vessel shall have due regard to the prevailing circumstances and conditions of restricted visibility when complying with the Rules of Section I of this Part.

(d) A vessel which detects by radar alone the presence of another vessel shall determine if a close-quarters situation is developing and/or risk of collision exists. If so, she shall take avoiding action in ample time, provided that when such action consists of an alteration of course, so far as possible the following shall be avoided:
(i) an alteration of course to port for a vessel forward of the beam, other than for a vessel being overtaken;
(ii) an alteration of course towards a vessel abeam or abaft the beam.
(e) Except where it has been determined that a risk of collision does not exist, every vessel which hears apparently forward of her beam the fog signal of another vessel, or which cannot avoid a close-quarters situation with another vessel forward of her beam, shall reduce her speed to the minimum at which she can be kept on her course. She shall if necessary take all her way off and in any event navigate with extreme caution until danger of collision is over.

PART C. LIGHTS AND SHAPES

RULE 20

Application
(a) Rules in this Part shall be complied with in all weathers.
(b) The Rules concerning lights shall be complied with from sunset to sunrise, and during such times no other lights shall be exhibited, except such lights as cannot be mistaken for the lights specified in these Rules or do not impair their visibility or distinctive character, or interfere with the keeping of a proper look-out.
(c) The lights prescribed by these Rules shall, if carried, also be exhibited from sunrise to sunset in restricted visibility and may be exhibited in all other circumstances when it is deemed necessary.
(d) The Rules concerning shapes shall be complied with by day.
(e) The lights and shapes specified in these Rules shall comply with the provisions of Annex I to these Regulations.

RULE 21

Definitions
(a) "Masthead light" means a white light placed over the fore and aft centreline of the vessel showing an unbroken light over an arc of the horizon of 225 degrees and so fixed as to show the light from right ahead to 22.5 degrees abaft the beam on either side of the vessel.
(b) "Sidelights" means a green light on the starboard side and a red light on the port side each showing an unbroken light over an arc of the horizon of 122.5 degrees and so fixed as to show the light from right ahead to 22.5 degrees abaft the beam on its respective side. In a vessel of less than 20 metres in length the sidelights may be combined in one lantern carried on the fore and aft centreline of the vessel.
(c) "Sternlight" means a white light placed as nearly as practicable at the stern showing an unbroken light over an arc of the horizon of 135 degrees and so fixed as to show the light 67.5 degrees from right aft on each side of the vessel.
(d) "Towing light" means a yellow light having the same characteristics as the "sternlight" defined in paragraph (c) of this Rule.

(e) "All round light" means a light showing an unbroken light over an arc of the horizon of 360 degrees.
(f) "Flashing light" means a light flashing at regular intervals at a frequency of 120 flashes or more per minute.

RULE 22

Visibility of lights
The lights prescribed in these Rules shall . . . be visible at the following minimum ranges:
(a) In vessels of 50 metres or more in length:
—a masthead light, 6 miles;
—a sidelight, 3 miles;
—a sternlight, 3 miles;
—a towing light, 3 miles;
—a white, red, green or yellow all-round light, 3 miles.
(b) In vessels of 12 metres or more in length but less than 50 metres in length:
—a masthead light, 5 miles; except that where the length of the vessel is less than 20 metres, 3 miles;
—a sidelight, 2 miles;
—a sternlight, 2 miles;
—a towing light, 2 miles;
—a white, red, green or yellow all-round light, 2 miles.
(c) In vessels of less than 12 metres in length:
—a masthead light, 2 miles;
—a sidelight, 1 mile;
—a sternlight, 2 miles;
—a towing light, 2 miles;
—a white, red, green or yellow all-round light, 2 miles.
(d) In inconspicuous, partly submerged vessels or objects being towed:
—a white all-round light, 3 miles.

RULE 23

Power-driven vessels underway
(a) A power-driven vessel underway shall exhibit:
(i) a masthead light forward;
(ii) a second masthead light abaft of and higher than the forward one; except that a vessel of less than 50 metres in length shall not be obliged to exhibit such light but may do so;
(iii) sidelights;
(iv) sternlights.
(b) An air-cushion vessel when operating in the non-displacement mode shall, in addition to the lights prescribed in paragraph (a) of this Rule, exhibit an all-round flashing yellow light.
(c) (i) A power-driven vessel of less than 12 metres in length may in lieu of the lights prescribed in paragraph (a) of this Rule exhibit an all-round white light and sidelights;
(ii) a power-driven vessel of less than 7 metres in length whose maximum speed does not exceed 7 knots may in lieu of the lights prescribed in paragraph (a) of this Rule exhibit an all-round white light and shall, if practicable, also exhibit sidelights;
(iii) the masthead light or all-round white light on a power-driven vessel of less than 12 metres in length may be displaced from the fore and aft centreline of the vessel if centreline fitting is not practicable, provided that the sidelights are combined in one lantern which shall be carried on the fore and aft centreline of the vessel or located as nearly as practicable in the same fore and aft line as the masthead light or the all-round white light.

RULE 24

Towing and pushing

(a) A power-driven vessel when towing shall exhibit.

    (i) instead of the light prescribed in Rule 23 (a) (i) or (a) (ii) two masthead lights forward in a vertical line. When the length of the tow, measuring from the stern of the towing vessel to the after end of the tow exceeds 200 metres, three such lights in a vertical line;

    (ii) sidelights;

    (iii) a sternlight;

    (iv) a towing light in a vertical line above the sternlight;

    (v) when the length of the tow exceeds 200 metres, a diamond shape where it can best be seen.

(b) When a pushing vessel and a vessel being pushed ahead are rigidly connected in a composite unit they shall be regarded as a power-driven vessel and exhibit the light prescribed in Rule 23.

(c) A power-driven vessel when pushing ahead or towing alongside, except in the case of a composite unit, shall exhibit:

    (i) instead of the light prescribed in Rule 23 (a) (i) or (a) (ii), two masthead lights forward in a vertical line;

    (ii) sidelights;

    (iii) a sternlight.

(d) A power-driven vessel to which paragraph (a) or (c) of this Rule applies shall also comply with Rule 23 (a) (i).

(e) A vessel or object being towed, other than those mentioned in paragraph (g) of the Rule, shall exhibit:

    (i) sidelights;

    (ii) a sternlight;

    (iii) when the length of the tow exceeds 200 metres, a diamond shape where it can best be seen.

(f) Provided that any number of vessels being towed alongside or pushed in a group shall be lighted as one vessel,

    (i) a vessel being pushed ahead, not being part of a composite unit, shall exhibit at the forward end, sidelights;

    (ii) a vessel being towed alongside shall exhibit a sternlight and at the forward end, sidelights.

(g) An inconspicuous partly submerged vessel or object, or combination of such vessels or objects being towed, shall exhibit:

    (i) if it is less than 25 metres in breadth, one all-round white light at or near the forward end and one at or near the after end except that dracones need not exhibit a light at or near the forward end;

    (ii) if it is 25 metres or more in breadth, two additional all-round white lights at or near the extremities of its breadth;

    (iii) if it exceeds 100 metres in length, additional all-round white lights between the lights prescribed in sub-paragraphs (i) and (ii) so that the distance between the lights shall not exceed 100 metres;

    (iv) a diamond shape at or near the aftermost extremity of the last vessel or object being towed and if the length of the tow exceeds 200 metres an additional diamond shape where it can best be seen and located as far forward as is practicable.

(h) Where from any sufficient cause it is impracticable for a vessel or object being towed to exhibit the lights or shapes prescribed in paragraph (e) or (g) of this Rule, all possible measures shall be taken to light the vessel or object towed or at least to indicate the presence of such vessel or object.

(i) Where from any sufficient cause it is impracticable for a vessel not normally engaged in towing operations to display the lights prescribed in paragraph (a) or (c) of this Rule, such vessel shall not be required to exhibit those lights when engaged in towing another vessel in distress or otherwise in need of assistance. All possible measures shall be taken to indicate the nature of the relationship between the towing vessel and the vessel being towed as authorised by Rule 36, in particular by illuminating the towline.

RULE 25

Sailing vessels underway and vessels under oars

(a) A sailing vessel underway shall exhibit:

    (i) sidelights;

    (ii) sternlights.

(b) In a sailing vessel of less than 20 metres in length the lights prescribed in paragraph (a) of this Rule may be combined in one lantern carried at or near the top of the mast where it can best be seen.

(c) A sailing vessel underway may, in addition to the lights prescribed in paragraph (a) of this Rule, exhibit at or near the top of the mast, where they can best be seen, two all-round lights in a vertical line, the upper being red and the lower green, but these lights shall not be exhibited in conjunction with the combined lantern permitted by paragraph (b) of this Rule.

(d) (i) A sailing vesel of less than 7 metres in length shall, if practicable, exhibit the lights prescribed in paragraph (a) or (b) of this Rule, but if she does not, she shall have ready at hand an electric torch or lighted lantern showing a white light which shall be exhibited in sufficient time to prevent collision.

    (ii) A vessel under oars may exhibit the lights prescribed in this Rule for sailing vessels, but if she does not, she shall have ready at hand an electric torch or lighted lantern showing a white light which shall be exhibited in sufficient time to prevent collision.

(e) A vessel proceeding under sail when also being propelled by machinery shall exhibit forward where it can best be seen a conical shape, apex downwards.

RULE 26

Fishing vessels

(a) A vessel engaged in fishing, whether underway or at anchor, shall exhibit only the lights and shapes prescribed in this Rule.

(b) A vessel when engaged in trawling, by which is meant the dragging through the water of a dredge net or other apparatus used as a fishing appliance, shall exhibit:

    (i) two all-round lights in a vertical line, the upper being green and the other white, or a shape consisting of two cones with their apexes together in a vertical line one above the other; a vessel may instead of this shape exhibit a basket;

    (ii) a masthead light abaft of and higher than the all-round green light; a vessel of less than 50 metres in length shall not be obliged to exhibit such a light but may do so;

    (iii) when making way through the water, in addition to the lights prescribed in this paragraph, sidelights and a sternlight.

(c) A vessel engaged in fishing, other than trawling, shall exhibit:

    (i) two all-round lights in a vertical line, the upper being red and the lower white, or a shape consisting of two cones with apexes together in a line one above the other; a vessel of less than 20 metres in length may instead of this shape exhibit a basket;

    (ii) when there is outlying gear extending more than 150 metres horizontally from the vessel, an all-round white light or a cone apex upwards in the direction of the gear;

    (iii) when making way through the water, in addition to the lights prescribed in this paragraph, sidelights and a sternlight.

(d) A vessel engaged in fishing in close proximity to other vessels engaged in fishing may exhibit the additional signals described in Annex II to these Regulations.

(e) A vessel when not engaged in fishing shall not exhibit the lights or shapes prescribed in this Rule, but only those prescribed for a vessel of her length.

RULE 27

Vessels not under command or restricted in their ability to manoeuvre

(a) A vessel not under command shall exhibit:

    (i) two all-round red lights in a vertical line where they can best be seen;

    (ii) two balls or similar shapes in a vertical line where they can best be seen;

    (iii) when making way through the water, in addition to the lights prescribed in this paragraph, sidelights and a sternlight.

(b) A vessel restricted in her ability to manoeuvre, except a vessel engaged in mine-clearance operations, shall exhibit:

    (i) three all-round lights in a vertical line where they can best be seen. The highest and lowest of these lights shall be red and the middle light shall be white;

    (ii) three shapes in a vertical line where they can best be seen. The highest and lowest of these shapes shall be balls and the middle one a diamond;

    (iii) when making way through the water, a masthead light or lights, sidelights and a sternlight, in addition to the lights prescribed in sub-paragraph (i);

    (iv) when at anchor, in addition to the lights or shapes prescribed in sub-paragraphs (i) and (ii), the light, lights or shape prescribed in Rule 30.

(c) A power-driven vessel engaged in a towing operation such as severely restricts the towing vessel and her tow in their ability to deviate from their course shall, in addition to the lights or shapes prescribed in Rule 24(a), exhibit the lights or shapes prescribed in sub-paragraphs (b) (i) and (ii) of this Rule.

(d) A vessel engaged in dredging or underwater operations, when restricted in her ability to manoeuvre, shall exhibit the lights and shapes prescribed in sub-paragraph (b), (ii) and (iii) of this Rule and shall in addition, when an obstruction exists, exhibit:

    (i) two all-round red lights or two balls in a vertical line to indicate the side on which the obstruction exists;

    (ii) two all-round green lights or two diamonds in a vertical line to indicate the side on which another vessel may pass;

    (iii) when at anchor, the lights or shapes prescribed in this paragraph instead of the lights or shape prescribed in Rule 30.

(e) Whenever the size of a vessel engaged in diving operations makes it impracticable to exhibit all lights and shapes prescribed in paragraph (d) of this Rule, the following shall be exhibited:

    (iv) three all-round lights in a vertical line where they can best be seen. The highest and lowest of these lights shall be red and the middle light shall be white;

    (ii) a rigid replica of the International Code flag ''A'' not less than 1 metre in height. Measures shall be taken to ensure its all-round visibility.

(f) A vessel engaged in mine-clearance operations

shall in addition to the lights prescribed for a power-driven vessel in Rule 23 or to the lights or shape prescribed for a vessel at anchor in Rule 30 as appropriate, exhibit three all-round green lights or three all-round balls. One of these lights or shapes shall be exhibited near the foremast head and one at each end of the fore yard. These lights or shapes indicate that it is dangerous for another vessel to approach within 1000 metres of the mine-clearance vessel.

(g) Vessels of less than 12 metres in length, except those engaged in diving operations, shall not be required to exhibit the lights and shapes prescribed in this Rule.

(h) The signals prescribed in this Rule are not signals of vessels in distress and requiring assistance.

RULE 28

Vessels constrained by their draft
A vessel constrained by her draft may, in addition to the lights prescribed for power-driven vessels in Rule 23, exhibit where they can best be seen three all-round red lights in a vertical line, or a cylinder.

RULE 29

Pilot vessels
(a) A vessel engaged on pilotage duty shall exhibit.
    (i) at or near the masthead, two all-round lights in a vertical line, the upper being white and the lower red;
    (ii) when underway, in addition, sidelights and a sternlight;
    (iii) when at anchor, in addition to the lights prescribed in sub-paragraph (i), the lights or shape prescribed in Rule 30 for vessels at anchor.
(b) A pilot vessel when not engaged on pilotage duty shall exhibit the lights or shapes prescribed for a similar vessel of her length.

RULE 30

Anchored vessels and vessels aground
(a) A vessel at anchor shall exhibit where it can best be seen:
    (i) in the fore part, an all-round white light or one ball;
    (ii) at or near the stern and at a lower level than the light prescribed in sub-paragraph (i), an all-round white light.
(b) A vessel of less than 50 metres in length may exhibit an all-round white light where it can best be seen instead of the lights prescribed in paragraph (a) of this Rule.
(c) A vessel at anchor may, and a vessel of 100 metres and more in length shall, also use the available working or equivalent lights to illuminate her decks.
(d) A vessel aground shall exhibit the lights prescribed in paragraph (a) or (b) of this Rule and in addition, where they can best be seen:
    (i) two all-round red lights in a vertical line;
    (ii) three balls in a vertical line.
(e) A vessel of less than 7 metres in length, when at anchor not in or near a narrow channel, fairway or anchorage, or where other vessels normally navigate, shall not be required to exhibit the lights or shape prescribed in paragraphs (a) and (b) of this Rule.
(f) A vessel of less than 12 metres in length, when aground, shall not be required to exhibit the lights or shapes prescribed in sub-paragraphs (d) (i) and (ii) of this Rule.

RULE 31

Seaplanes
Where it is impracticable for a seaplane to exhibit lights and shapes of the characteristics or in the positions prescribed in the Rules of this Part she shall exhibit lights and shapes as closely similar in characteristics and position as is possible.

PART D. SOUND AND LIGHT SIGNALS

RULE 32

Definitions
(a) The word "whistle" means any sound signalling appliance capable of producing the prescribed blasts and which complies with the specifications in Annex III to these Regulations.
(b) The term "short blast" means a blast of about one second's duration.
(c) The term "prolonged blast" means a blast of from four to six seconds' duration.

RULE 33

Equipment for sound signals
(a) A vessel of 12 metres or more in length shall be provided with a whistle and a bell and a vessel of 100 metres or more in length shall, in addition, be provided with a gong, the tone and sound of which cannot be confused with that of the bell. The whistle, bell and gong shall comply with the specifications in Annex III to these Regulations (not reproduced here). The bell or gong or both may be replaced by other equipment having the same respective sound characteristics, provided that manual sounding of the prescribed signals shall always be possible.
(b) A vessel of less than 12 metres in length shall not be obliged to carry the sound signalling appliances prescribed in paragraph (a) of this Rule but if she does not, she shall be provided with some other means of making an efficient sound signal.

RULE 34

Manoeuvring and warning signals
(a) When vessels are in sight of one another, a power-driven vessel underway, when manoeuvring as authorised or required by these Rules, shall indicate that manoeuvre by the following signals on her whistle:
    —one short blast to mean "I am altering my course to starboard";
    —two short blasts to mean "I am altering my course to port";
    —three short blasts to mean "I am operating astern propulsion".
(b) Any vessel may supplement the whistle signals prescribed in paragraph (a) of this Rule by light signals, repeated as appropriate, whilst the manoeuvre is being carried out:
    (i) these light signals shall have the following significance:
    —one flash to mean "I am altering my course to starboard";
    —two flashes to mean "I am altering my course to port";
    —three flashes to mean "I am operating astern propulsion";

    (ii) the duration of each flash shall be about one second, the interval between flashes shall be about one second, and the interval between successive signals shall be not less than ten seconds;
    (iii) the light used for this signal shall, if fitted, be an all-round white light, visible at a minimum range of 5 miles, and shall comply with the provisions of Annex I to these Regulations (not reproduced here).
(c) When in sight of one another in a narrow channel or fairway:
    (i) a vessel intending to overtake another shall in compliance with Rule 9 (e) (i) indicate her intention by the following signals on her whistle:
    —two prolonged blasts followed by one short blast to mean "I intend to overtake you on your starboard side";
    —two prolonged blasts followed by two short blasts to mean "I intend to overtake you on your port side".
    (ii) the vessel about to be overtaken when acting in accordance with Rule 9 (e) (i) shall indicate her agreement by the following signal on her whistle:
    —one prolonged, one short, one prolonged and one short blast in that order.
(d) When vessels in sight of one another are approaching each other and from any cause either vessel fails to understand the intentions or actions of the other, or is in doubt whether sufficient action is being taken by the other to avoid collision, the vessel in doubt shall immediately indicate such doubt by giving at least five short and rapid blasts on the whistle. Such signal may be supplemented by a light signal of at least five short and rapid flashes.
(e) A vessel nearing a bend or an area of a channel or fairway where other vessels may be obscured by an intervening obstruction shall sound one prolonged blast. Such signal shall be answered with a prolonged blast by any approaching vessel that may be within hearing around the bend or behind the intervening obstruction.
(f) If whistles are fitted on a vessel at a distance apart of more than 100 metres, one whistle only shall be used for giving manoeuvring and warning signals.

RULE 35

Sound signals in restricted visibility
In or near an area of restricted visibility, whether by day or night, the signals prescribed in this Rule shall be used as follows:
(a) A power-driven vessel making way through the water shall sound at intervals of not more than 2 minutes one prolonged blast.
(b) A power-driven vessel underway but stopped and making no way through the water shall sound at intervals of not more than 2 minutes two prolonged blasts in succession with an intervals of about 2 seconds between them.
(c) A vessel not under command, a vessel restricted in her ability to manoeuvre, a vessel constrained by her draft, a sailing vessel, a vessel engaged in fishing and a vessel engaged in towing or pushing another vessel shall, instead of the signals prescribed in paragraphs (a) or (b) of this Rule, sound at intervals of not more than 2 minutes three blasts in succession, namely one prolonged followed by two short blasts.
(d) A vessel engaged in fishing, when at anchor, and a vessel restricted in her ability to manoeuvre when carrying out her work at anchor, shall instead of the signals prescribed in paragraph (g) of this Rule sound the signal prescribed in paragraph (c) of this Rule.
(e) A vessel towed or if more than one vessel is

towed the last vessel of the tow, if manned, shall at intervals of not more than 2 minutes sound four blasts in succession, namely one prolonged followed by three short blasts. When practicable, this signal shall be made immediately after the signal made by the towing vessel.

(f) When a pushing vessel and a vessel being pushed ahead are rigidly connected in a composite unit they shall be regarded as a power-driven vessel and shall give the signals prescribed in paragraphs (a) or (b) of this Rule.

(g) A vessel at anchor shall at intervals of not more than one minute ring the bell rapidly for about 5 seconds. In a vessel of 100 metres or more in length the bell shall be sounded in the forepart of the vessel and immediately after the ringing of the bell the gong shall be sounded rapidly for about 5 seconds in the after part of the vessel. A vessel at anchor may in addition sound three blasts in succession, namely one short, one prolonged and one short blast, to give warning of her position and of the possibility of collision to an approaching vessel.

(h) A vessel aground shall give the bell signal and if required the gong signal prescribed in paragraph (g) of this Rule and shall, in addition, give three separate and distinct strokes on the bell immediately before and after the rapid ringing of the bell. A vessel aground may in addition sound an appropriate whistle signal.

(i) A vessel of less than 12 metres in length shall not be obliged to give the above-mentioned signals but, if she does not, shall make some other efficient sound signal at intervals of not more than 2 minutes.

(j) A pilot vessel when engaged on pilotage duty may in addition to the signals prescribed in paragraphs (a), (b) or (g) of this Rule sound an identity signal consisting of four short blasts.

RULE 36

Signals to attract attention
If necessary to attract the attention of another vessel any vessel may make light or sound signals that cannot be mistaken for any signal authorised elsewhere in these Rules, or may direct the beam of her searchlight in the direction of the danger, in such a way as not to embarrass any vessel.

Any light to attract the attention of another vessel shall be such that it cannot be mistaken for any aid to navigation. For the purpose of this Rule the use of high intensity intermittent or revolving lights, such as strobe lights, shall be avoided.

RULE 37

Distress signals
When a vessel is in distress and requires assistance she shall use or exhibit the signals described in Annex IV to these Regulations (not reproduced here).